To My Parents

Counter-clockwise from top: John R. Mott, sophomore at Cornell University; Robert E. Speer, entering Princeton University, and Robert P. Wilder, senior, Princeton University, 1886.

THE CREATION OF A STUDENT MOVEMENT TO EVANGELIZE THE WORLD

A History and Analysis of the Early
Stages of the Student Volunteer
Movement for Foreign Missions

TIMOTHY C. WALLSTROM

William Carey International
University Press
1539 E. HOWARD STREET, PASADENA, CA 91104

International Standard Book Number 0-86585-000-3
Library of Congress Catalog Number 80-66254

Published by

The William Carey International University Press
1539 East Howard Street
Pasadena, California 91104, U.S.A.

(213) 797-0533

PRINTED IN THE UNITED STATES OF AMERICA

Contents

Preface

This book was written out of a desire to familiarize both myself and other students of the 1980s with the origins of a vast and ambitious student missionary undertaking begun in the 1880s. Any student interested in world evangelism will find that much can be learned from a backwards glance at the work of his predecessors. Other individuals, student and otherwise, Christian and non-Christian, will be amazed at the commitment of life and energy to this formidable endeavor — the preaching of the gospel to every individual within a generation. Here was a handful of college students trying to bring to completion a task with which the church had been struggling for two millenia. And making progress.

I have thought it wise, in this brief account, to restrict my attention to the creative stage of the Student Volunteer Movement's development. During this period alone was the Movement solely under the direction of students from a single era; moreover, these were the students who cast the Movement into the shape it was to retain for at least a generation.

I have made no effort either to evaluate the significance of the Movement in the larger context, or to study the social attitudes of the student volunteers, since both of these topics can only be handled properly in a broader and more comprehensive work. Nor have I made any attempt to critically analyze the organizational structure of the Movement, since the Movement's decline would prove immeasurably more instructive on this point than the Movement's creation.

I would like to express my appreciation to my friends at the United States Center for World Mission and the Institute for International Studies, for their assistance and common interest in this project.

> Timothy C. Wallstrom
> Pasadena, California
> January 15, 1980

1
The Student Volunteer Movement — An Introduction

Has any such offering of living young men and women been presented in our age, in our country, in any age or in any country since the days of Pentecost?
— President McCosh of Princeton College, May, 1887[1]

The time an individual spends in college often has a tremendous impact on the course of his later life. What he learns and what he does not learn, what he experiences and does not experience, what opportunities he discovers and fails to discover, what he comes to believe and what he comes to doubt, all influence in a vital way the career decisions he will need to make during and after his time in school. The environment in which a student spends his college days works to condition his world view and thus to delineate and clarify his personal horizons. As he begins his life work, he can only direct himself towards those horizons which are, for him, visible.

In this light, the prospects for any significant commitment of American students to mission work have rarely looked gloomier than during the years of the late eighteenth and early nineteenth centuries, eighty to one hundred years before the Student Volunteer Movement came into being. Mission opportunities were not only *unknown* to college students, they did not exist at all. In fact, North American churches had at their disposal not a single agency for sending Christian servants to foreign lands. The typical environment to which a college student was exposed, moreover, did little to encourage him to create his own opportunities. For in the early nineteenth century the American institutions of higher education were besieged by the rationalistic and materialistic philosophies of the French Enlightenment, much to the detriment of collegiate Christian life. "It became the fashion for students to scoff at the forms of religion as the 'shackles of superstition.' "[2]

When, therefore, the annals of the early 1800s reveal that a small band of students at Williams College dedicated their lives to foreign missions, the historically alert reader will no doubt raise an eyebrow. He may well raise both eyebrows if he reads on to discover in the waning decades of that same nineteenth century the emergence of a widespread and substantial mission movement in the colleges: a movement conceived of, organized by, and motivated by some of the most capable students the finest Eastern schools could produce; and more importantly, a movement whose substance and strength was sacrificially provided out of the flesh and blood of Christian students. Such was the Student Volunteer Movement for Foreign Missions, organized in 1888 and an important instrument in recruiting missionary candidates and promoting mission work for at least a generation.

The Student Volunteer Movement (SVM) was comprised of students in the United States and Canada who had declared it to be their purpose, if God permit, to become missionaries in foreign lands, uniting themselves by a rallying cry or "watchword" which called for "The Evangelization of the World in This Generation." The uprising began quietly in the living room of a retired missionary, whose likewise mission-minded son was an underclassman at a nearby college in New Jersey. This young man, whose name was Robert Wilder, banded together with a small number of his classmates of declared missionary intentions, meeting each week for inspiration and instruction. For two and a half years this band continued to flourish; but it made no apparent efforts to extend itself beyond the walls of this one institution. From the viewpoint of a casual retrospective, it appears remarkable that such an extension ever took place. Robert Wilder had to be individually persuaded to attend the intercollegiate Mount Hermon summer school in 1886; and the evangelist who presided there that summer, though highly renowned, was quite ignorant of mission concerns. Yet the two hundred fifty delegates assembled at Mount Hermon were to see the birth of a movement, as the little band of New Jersey students took intercollegiate root. Twenty years later almost 3,000 volunteers had sailed as missionaries to foreign lands; thousands more, who had volunteered but were for various reasons unable to go, were supporting the

Time Line of Sailed Volunteers

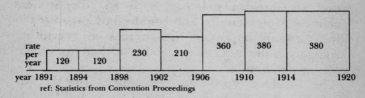

ref: Statistics from Convention Proceedings

mission effort with their prayers and their pocketbooks. And the Movement was only then beginning to enter what was to be numerically its period of greatest vitality: in the twenty years from 1900 to 1920 more than twice this many sailed, and volunteers were leaving for the mission fields at the rate of almost one each day.

This booklet will endeavor to provide the reader with an understanding of the origin and early characteristics of the Student Volunteer Movement for Foreign Missions. Soon we shall trace the historical developments which transformed the unpromising environment just described into one in which the SVM could flourish. But before tracing the Movement's ancestry, its birth and childhood, its adolescence and its entry into maturity, let us shake hands with the Movement in its adulthood, meeting it in the same manner as did the college students a century ago. The Movement greeted these students with an appeal to missionary service, and the power of this encounter irrevocably redirected the course of many a life.

2
The Volunteer Appeal

Many of the students volunteering as missionaries would have been virtually assured of profitable employment in secular fields by merit of their intelligence and abilities. Among the volunteers were some of the most able and gifted students of the age, and even those of more modest faculties could anticipate the comfortable positions to which a college diploma, then more than today, entitled its owner. What kind of appeal was required — what facts needed to be marshalled, what kind of opportunities envisioned, what types of challenges presented — to help persuade thousands of young men and women to give up promising careers as perhaps businessmen, physicians, scientists, or engineers, in order to sail to the earth's remote corners in the lowly esteemed capacity of a missionary?

Personal example was a most important aspect of the

missionary appeal. The student volunteer was a colleague, a peer, an equal in age and ability, who had already taken the foolish step he was advocating. He could therefore encourage his companions to "come," a much more persuasive request than "go." Typically, a volunteer's appeal would emphasize the following ideas.

The Need

"Over one thousand millions," exclaimed John Mott, the longtime chairman of the SVM. "Can we grasp the number? No, indeed! . . . Not only the Scriptures but scientific observation prove . . . that those people without Christ have a need which is very deep. Think of them tonight, living in darkness and ignorance, steeped in superstition and idolatry, in degradation and corruption."[1] Before declaring his intention to become a missionary, a young Princeton student who was to spend forty years as a missionary in Japan, rose to lament, "Woe is me if I preach not the gospel to the heathen." John Forman, a fellow undergraduate immediately contributed: "I know what ails Curtis, he sleeps under a chart containing 856 black squares representing 856 million heathen and 170 green squares representing 170 million Mohammedans. Anyone sleeping under a chart like that must decide to be a missionary or have a nightmare every night of the week."[2] According to the volunteers, the need for Christ was felt by every living individual, wherever he might live. If religion had any validity, they argued, it must be valid for all men, regardless of their racial or geographical heritage. Because each individual had a spiritual need which could be met only by Christ, every human being needed to be told of Christ and his gospel. The non-Christian alternatives, moreover, were seen as cruelly inadequate to meet even the social needs of foreign peoples.

Not only was this need great and universal, but it was an urgent need as well. Volunteers emphasized that only the present generation was capable of reaching its contemporaries, and that each day thousands of the unreached slipped haplessly and irretrievably into eternal oblivion. Furthermore, a neglect of missions by the present generation would make more difficult the task of succeeding generations. The uncertain future of the opportunities hinging on political comings and goings helped to heighten this sense of urgency.

The Opportunity

The student volunteers saw their age as one of unprecedented opportunity. "The world is better known and more accessible than in any other generation which has ever lived. The need of the world is more articulate and intelligible than it has ever been, and the resources of the Church are far greater today than has been the case in any preceding generation."[3] The unequalled opportunities they perceived led them to work for and anticipate unprecedented success.

Volunteers exulted in the opportunities made possible by the acquisition of geographical and cultural knowledge and the advances in communication and transportation, products of the technology and industry of the nineteenth century. "Science is the handmaid to piety in these days," declared Rev. A.T. Pierson at the 1891 Convention of the SVM. "She offers us every facility . . . to accomplish this warfare of the ages." "Lightning and steam have yoked themselves to the chariot of the Church of God, and the chariot of God's church can speed where she will."[4] The human and financial resources of the American Protestant church were also enthusiastically illuminated. The volunteers argued that with 10,000,000 Protestant Christians in the United

States alone, possessing a wealth in excess $12,000,000,000 (in 1890 dollars!), the evangelization of the world should be possible within a generation.[5] These opportunities will be further discussed in a subsequent chapter.

The Obligation

"It would seem to me," commented SVM Chairman John Mott, "that every Christian of reality ought to be a missionary Christian; for, as Archbishop Whately has said — mark his language, note it well: 'If my faith be false, I ought to change it; whereas if it be true, I am bound to propagate it.' There is no middle ground; either abandon my religion or be a missionary in spirit."[6] The Student Volunteer Movement was rooted in the conviction that "every one of us rests under a sort of obligation to give life and time and possession to the evangelization of the souls everywhere that have never heard of Jesus Christ, and we are bound to go, unless we can offer some sure ground of exemption."[7]

The most fundamental and important justification for perceiving the missionary enterprise as an obligation of both the church and the individual was provided by the Holy Scriptures. "The Great Commission of Christ . . . clearly expresses our obligation to make Christ known to all men . . . it was intended . . . for all time and for each Christian in his own time."[8] It was frequently referred to as the Last Command of Jesus Christ. The obligation to tell others of Christ was based also on ethical grounds. "You have no right to hear and believe without testifying," warned Dr. A.T. Pierson at a early SVM Convention.[9] By withholding from others the knowledge which gives life its meaning, one actually transgresses against those from whom this knowledge is kept. "Every

Chinese, every East Indian, every inhabitant of the southern seas, has the right to know the mission of Jesus Christ, and you and I violate the eighth commandment if we keep this knowledge from them . . . What a colossal crime against two-thirds of the human race to withhold this surpassing knowledge!"[10] The urgent need of the world and the unprecedented opportunities for its evangelization, which were discussed in the preceding sections, worked to intensify the missionary obligation. "You and I cannot excuse ourselves by doing what our fathers did . . . We have the opportunity to do larger things, and we are going to be judged by our talents and the use of them."[11]

"Suppose then that the individual Christian does have an obligation to tell others of Christ," a student might respond, "why must he go overseas to do so? Is there not ample need at home?" The volunteers answered this objection in two ways. First, because the missionary effort is so patently an enterprise of faith, its maintenance will indeed exercise and strengthen the spiritual vitality of the home church, much as the use of the bodily extremities will exercise and strengthen the heart which supplies them with blood. Missions do not sap the vigor of the home base; they fortify it. Second, and more pointedly, the greater need and smaller resources of the "non-Christian nations" entitled them to greater priority. "If it is a good thing to go where we are needed, it is more Christlike to go where we are needed most."[12]

The individual obligation to minister overseas was in fact a simply corollary of this greater need; no special call was considered necessary. Robert Wilder, one of the Movement's originators, found "nothing in the Bible to indicate that a man needs more of a call to take him to Africa than to Dakota."[13] The whole of a Christian's existence was held to be consecrated to the service of his Master, and the sole remaining question involved the means through which that service could be most effectively rendered. In the presence of a specific command and an urgent need to minister abroad, volunteers believed the duty rested with the individual to show that his life might be used more effectively in other ways. It was not God's responsibility to push him in the direction to which He had already pointed. Volunteers believed the Christian attitude to the missionary call should be not "why?" but "why not?" "While vast continents are shrouded in almost utter darkness, and hundreds of millions suffer the horrors of heathenism and Islam, the burden of proof lies upon you to show that the circumstances in which God has placed you were meant by Him to keep you out of the foreign field."[14]

What kind of circumstances would suffice to exempt the Christian from this presumptive obligation? Certainly not a love of home and family, nor a desire for the good life. "Let Jesus Christ answer . . . 'He that hateth not his father and his mother, and his brother and his sister, yea, and his own life also, he cannot be my disciple.' "[15] Would the mastery of a profession such as medicine, law, or teaching constitute an exemption? Again, certainly not, when there is a surfeit of such professionals at home and a tragic dearth abroad. Because the "non-Christian lands" stood in greater need in practically every conceivable category, there was probably no general class of individuals which by possession of some training or skill would be considered by the volunteers exempt. Nevertheless, they maintained that certain individuals would be called by God to stay at home, either because of some gift or opportunity unique to themselves, or simply in keeping with the inscrutable will of the Omniscient.

Volunteers did not advocate a total neglect of the home base.

The Challenge

"The Evangelization of the World in This Generation" — such was the challenge and the watchword of the Student Volunteer Movement for Foreign Missions. Robert Speer, a volunteer of exceptional ability from Princeton College, explained this phrase at the 1891 Cleveland Convention. "We do not mean the *conversion* of the world . . . Nor, in the second place, do I think any of the volunteers mean the *Christianization* of the world . . . We do mean, however, that every intelligent, thoughtful, sincere volunteer believes and prays for the evangelization of the world before we die, and by that simple phrase is meant simply this: the presenting of the gospel in such a manner to every soul in this world that the responsibility for what is done with it shall no longer rest upon the Christian Church or on any individual Christian, but shall rest on each man's head for himself."[16] The world's "evangelization" was not meant to imply either the conversion of the world or the permeation of the world with Christian ideals and culture, and the Movement's leadership emphasized this repeatedly.

The appeal of the watchword functioned on two distinct levels. First, it was a call to obligation. The watchword summarized in pithy and striking fashion the mandate to answer an urgent and universal need. Since no individual or era could actively witness to the members of either a previous or future age, the broadest possible field in which one might discharge his responsibility was that of his contemporaries, those living "in this generation." Moreover, the inhabitants of a given era could *only* be reached by those of the same generation. The watchword represented the volunteer's interpretation of the way in which the duty of the Great Commission applied to a given generation, or individual within that generation. It "simply translates Christ's last command into terms of obligation concerning our lifetime,"[17] calling upon the individual Christian to perceive and carry out his evangelistic duty in as extensive a frame as permitted to him, both in space — "the world," and in time — "this generation."

But the watchword functioned as much more than a sterile call to obligation. Had it been perceived as merely an impractical goal, a vision, the statement of an appealing but impossible dream, it could never have become the rallying cry of such a movement. "The evangelization of the world in this generation is possible," averred the student volunteers, and this conviction was a crucial part of their appeal. Why, after all, was the language of the watchword preferable to that of the Great Commission, originally stated? Because the watchword mapped out a challenge. How does one tap the energy and commitment of college students? "I will tell you the way to do it," explained John Mott in his middle years, "and that is to place something before them which is tremendously difficult."[18] Thousands of college men and women responded to this challenge with all the enthusiasm, vitality, and vision of their youthful idealism, and with some of its naivete as well. As much as it was a challenge, however, the watchword remained equally a call to duty. The phrase, 'The Evangelization of the World in This Generation,' thus encapsulated an ingenious fusion of obligation and opportunity, and provided a powerful, succinct expression of the Movement's focus and appeal.

The Commitment

The process of becoming a volunteer began with the awareness of the obligation and opportunity to answer an urgent worldwide need. A student at an institution of higher learning could become a volunteer by signing the following declaration: "It is my purpose, if God permit, to become a foreign missionary." In so doing, the student indicated that he had set aside all aspirations for other employment and had committed himself to becoming a missionary overseas, unless God blocked his way. He was henceforth to consider the remaining time in his homeland as a period of preparation for his life's calling, structuring his education and activities accordingly. If God did prevent his departure, the volunteer was expected to provide financial, moral and spiritual support for his companions who succeeded in reaching the field.

What did it mean for God to "block the way"? A few situations were seen as clear evidence of divine guidance. Occasionally a volunteer would suddenly find himself burdened with the care of his parents or brothers and sisters and this qualified him for exemption. The volunteer suffering from ill health was encouraged to let the mission board decide whether this excuse was valid in his case. (Death was *always* perceived as a legitimate excuse!) If God manifestly directed the volunteer into another endeavor, other volunteers had no grounds to quarrel, but caveats were frequently issued. Inheriting a family business did not necessarily reveal the restraining hand of God. Only when the volunteer's alternative occupation would allow him to be of greater service to God was it deemed admissible for him to abandon his missionary intentions. The SVM, of course, had no power beyond that of moral suasion to enforce these guidelines.

But what function could this declaration possibly serve if "there is a general obligation resting upon Christian men" to preach the gospel to the world, and we already need "a special call to exempt us from its application to our lives?"[19] Why is a special commitment required when a special call is not? A volunteer would have replied that the declaration implied not only a recognition of obligation, but a commitment of the heart and the will to live in accordance with that obligation. The signing of the declaration itself was, after all, a perfectly voluntary action. By willingly signing such a document, the student hoped to cement in place his missionary purpose, to rivet his convictions until such time as he could apply to the mission boards. The commitment of life had been made when the declaration had been signed; the student now entered a period of preparation under the guidance and supervision of the Student Volunteer Movement.

3
Streams of Genesis

Having briefly surveyed the desert landscape of the American colleges of 1800, one is compelled to ponder how, by the year 1900, these same colleges could become the source from which this constant and committed stream of missionary volunteers did in fact flow. What changes must have been brought about in the colleges and universities during this momentous century; what men, what movements, what institutions and organizations must have come into existence; what shifts in mentality and emphasis must have taken place in order to make possible by the 1880's the Student Volunteer Movement? The effort to understand these questions, working forward in time from a point in the sufficiently distant past, is an activity not unlike the reading of a short story, for different streams from unrelated sources, responding only to the downward pull of gravity and the local geography, flow inexorably and sometimes spectacularly to a common climax. The gentle brooks, the rushing torrents, the misty waterfalls and angry cataracts, all will be carefully explored as we hike towards the site of their confluence, the Mount Hermon Conference of 1886. So many of the streams which contributed to the formation of the Student Volunteer Movement can be traced to that pioneer of American missions, Samuel J. Mills, to the Haystack Prayer Meeting, and to the events and organizations which followed soon after, that the SVM can be only marginally understood outside of this context. And so it is with Mills we shall begin our journey.

Samuel Mills and the Brethren Society

As an entering Freshman at Williams College in April of 1806, Samuel J. Mills, Jr., cut anything but an impressive figure. Mills was described by one of his roommates as having "an awkward figure and ungainly manner and an inelastic and croaking sort of voice."[1] But the situation was even more discouraging than it seemed, for although no one could have known it at the time, scarcely a dozen years remained to Mills' short life. In this context, his achievements are truly remarkable.[2]

The son of a Connecticut clergyman and a devout Christian mother, Mills came to Williams College with a developed interest in foreign missions as well as a firm Christian commitment. Soon after his arrival he came into contact with a group of fellow Christians who were meeting in prayer for a revival among the students at Williams College. Fearful of contempt and possible disruption from their peers, the group met in the countryside some distance from the college. Although he was but a freshman, he was also twenty-three; and because of his maturity and "the depth and sincerity of his own religious life," Mills quickly became the leader of these students.

The group continued to meet on a twice-weekly basis throughout the summer. One hot and sultry August afternoon, as five members of the band were meeting in a maple grove, the skies began to darken and the accompanying thundershowers and lightning persuaded them to return to the shelter of the college buildings. Before they could reach the campus, however, the clouds began to disperse, and they were able to continue their meeting under the shelter of a nearby haystack. Mills proceeded to direct the discussion towards the topic of foreign missions, contending that the Christianization of certain groups of people, such as those of Asia, would not take place so long as the students of Christian lands were unwilling to dedicate their lives to foreign evangelization. After some discussion, Mills invited the other students to join with him in offering their lives to the cause of foreign missions, so as to reach these unprivileged peoples. "We can do this if we will," he said, revealing a determination lacking from the expected "We will do this if we can." This Haystack Prayer Meeting, now commemorated by the Haystack Monument, led to the consecration of the first American student volunteers for foreign missions, the predecessors and in a very real sense the progenitors of the Student Volunteers of the end of the century.

This small band, with its now firmly established missionary emphasis, continued to meet during the next two years, drawing others (including the valedictorian of the class of 1809) into the fold of missionary commitment. On September 7, 1808, the group was officially organized, calling themselves simply the "Society of the Brethren," after two abortive attempts to give the society a Latin name. Its stated object was "to effect in the

persons of its members a mission or missions to the
heathen," and each member was to "keep absolutely free
from every engagement, which, after his prayerful
attention, and after consultation with the brethren, shall
be deemed incompatible with the object of this society."
New members took an oath to keep secret the very
existence of the society, a caution the Brethren deemed
necessary because of the then unfavorable attitude of the
Church towards missions and out of fear that they might
fail in their attempt to reach the mission field. The
Brethren were extremely cautious in admitting new
members, and their care is reflected in the high
proportion — approximately one-half — of members
seeing foreign missionary service. A sense of close
fraternity resulted from the secrecy of this band and the
common conviction among its members.[3]

The society was effectively transferred to Andover
Theological Seminary in 1810 when Mills and several
other members of the Brethren left Williams to
undertake further studies at Andover. The Society of the
Brethren remained active at Andover for fully sixty
years, its last recorded meeting being held in December
of 1870. What was perhaps the most direct link between
this Society and the Student Volunteer Movement was
provided in the person of Royal Gould Wilder, a member
of the Andover Brethren who set sail for India in 1846.
We shall encounter him again soon.

Efforts at Outreach

In attempting to transmit the gospel to foreign lands,
Mills and his colleagues were confronted with the
problem of finding both the volunteers necessary for
such a task and the means to send these volunteers
overseas. Concerning the problem of support, some of

the men suggested applying to the newly established London Missionary Society, but Mills firmly rejected this idea, convinced that the American churches ought to have their own sending agency. To possess their own conduit, however, Mills and his companions would need to trench it out by the force of their own muscle, and their efforts over the years were many and strenuous. In June, 1810, Mills and three others presented a petition to the General Association of the Congregational Churches of Massachusetts, asking that means be provided for sending them abroad. This petition had its desired impact, and by 1812, five young missionaries had set sail for Calcutta, India, under the auspices of what was soon to become the American Board of Commissioners for Foreign Missions (ABCFM). (Initially, the ABCFM was an interdenominational association of mission benefactors. Soon however, stimulated at least in part by the creation of the ABCFM, main line denominations began to form their own mission boards: between 1812 and 1817, for example, Baptist, Methodist and Episcopalian mission societies were formed. With the proliferation of denominational sending societies, the ABCFM became by 1860 the instrument of the Congregational Church alone.)[4]

In order to recruit more candidates for mission work, the members of the Brethren made efforts to introduce similar societies into other institutions. One member transferred to Middlebury College and Mills himself seriously considered transferring to Yale. But little tangible progress greeted these efforts. Attempts to introduce the society into Union and Dartmouth colleges met with failure. The Society of the Brethren never became intercollegiate to any significant degree, although a few branch societies seemed to have developed, and it may have persisted for a certain time at Williams College after Mills and others had left for Andover.

While at Andover, however, Mills and others founded a different organization which did spread, and consequently had perhaps an even greater impact on student missionary concern than the Society of the Brethren. This was the Andover "Society of Inquiry on the Subject of Missions," founded in early 1811. A majority of the early Brethren also belonged to the Society of Inquiry, so these two distinct societies were clearly not seen as redundant. The Society of Inquiry's members were required to be students of professed Christian conviction, sympathetic to the cause of missions. Its object was to "inquire into the state of the Heathen; the duty and importance of missionary labors; the best manner of conducting missions, and the most eligible places for their establishment."[5] In the early nineteenth century, Andover Theological Seminary was a key defensive stronghold for the beleaguered forces of evangelical Christianity. The vitality of the missionary interest promoted by the Society of Inquiry resulted in a fortuitous fusion of missionary concern with evangelical belief at Andover, pregnant with intercollegiate implications; for as the awakenings of the early nineteenth century helped to bring about an increase in evangelical belief, Andover provided leadership, assistance and an example to newly born collegiate religious societies. From 1811 to the time of the Civil War, scores of religious societies sprung up in the nation's colleges, many with a missionary emphasis.

One such society was the Philadelphian Society at Princeton College, founded in 1825, whose constitution designated that the first meeting of each month be set aside for discussion of missions.[6] In a remarkably indirect fashion, the formation of the Philadelphian Society can be traced to the original Society of the Brethren. A pamphlet written by two of the Brethren was left by a patient in the waiting room of a physician, who, upon reading the pamphlet, was persuaded to dedicate his medical skills to the work of the mission field. As he set sail for India, a young clerk standing on the dock was greatly moved by his example, and decided to enter Princeton College in preparation for missionary service. There he met up with another student of similar priorities; and together they founded the Philadelphian Society, which remained an important religious group on the Princeton campus for many decades. The early history of the SVM is inextricably intertwined with the activities of the Philadelphian Society, as we shall soon see.

Samuel J. Mills, Jr., died in 1818 at the age of 35, the victim of an illness contracted during an exploratory journey to Africa. According to the historian C.P. Shedd, "it is doubtful if any American ever exerted so great an influence in the cause of missions."[8] As mentioned, Mills was a primary initiator of the first American missionary sending society; and through the Society of the Brethren, the Society of Missionary Inquiry, and the numerous collegiate associations which began to give increased attention to missions, Mills did a great deal to arouse interest in missions and recruit mission candidates, particularly among the colleges. Mills and his colleagues, however, met with failure in one of their most cherished ambitions: the establishment of an intercollegiate association of societies dedicated to missionary concerns. The Society of the Brethren never became intercollegiate, and although Societies of Missionary Inquiry became widespread, these societies were unable to bind themselves together through any kind of overarching framework. The record of correspondence between the societies of different colleges reveals a tremendous desire for intercollegiate fellowship and unity, but the times were unfavorable for such an arrangement. In the days of the Williams Brethren, there were no more than twenty-five colleges in the country, most of which had student bodies smaller than one hundred. Communication between these colleges was slow and undependable, and transportation was a struggle today's jet-setter can scarcely appreciate. As a result, scattered pools of missionary interest remained in isolation, unable either to refresh each other or to flow into new and unwatered regions. The resources and development of the period were simply not adequate to engineer a connective network. With the passing of time, however, a British development was able to lay the groundwork necessary for such a matrix.

The Intercollegiate YMCA Movement

In June of 1844, the Young Men's Christian Association (YMCA) was founded in the inauspicious setting of a London dry goods establishment. George Williams and eleven fellow clerks were not consciously designing the prototype of an organization which was to see worldwide dissemination in but a few decades; they were merely responding to an obligation to take Christianity into the marketplace and into the everyday life of the urban world. Members maintained that "the supreme aim of your daily life should be to bring glory to your Redeemer, and that the most appropriate sphere for the attainment of this object is that of your daily calling." The emphasis was on carrying out the implications of Christianity in its social context, not on quibbling over some abstract theological doctrine, as had been the practice in many of the religious debating societies earlier in the century. Clearly, there was tremendous need for this type of emphasis, for the next decade saw the rapid spread of YMCAs throughout England, the United States, and several other countries, including Ireland, Scotland, Switzerland, Germany, and France.

The first collegiate YMCA in the United States appears to have been formed at the University of Virginia in 1858. Over the next two decades at least fifty YMCAs were organized within the nation's colleges, many springing up independently, unaware of the existence of other collegiate YMCAs, and many appropriating the name without tying themselves into the YMCA's International Committee.[9] The growth of the YMCAs within the colleges was to furnish the occasion for the establishment of an intercollegiate organization.

When Luther De Loraine Wishard transferred into Princeton College in September of 1875, the Philadelphian Society had just completed the celebration of its semi-centennial, and continued to dominate the religious life of the College. Although this young man was pleased with the religious vitality therein expressed, he was nevertheless disappointed to find that there was no YMCA at Princeton. At Hanover College in Indiana, he had not only participated actively in the student YMCA, but in 1872 had been its representative at the International Convention of the YMCA in Lowell, Massachusetts. Familiar with the resources at the YMCA's disposal, Wishard believed the Philadelphian Society would have much to gain by associating itself with this growing organization. Largely as a result of Wishard's efforts, who became its president in 1876, the

Philadelphian Society became a chapter of the YMCA through minor alterations in the Society's constitution. Princeton College and Luther Wishard now began to take the lead in the establishment of the Intercollegiate Young Men's Christian Association Movement (IYMCAM).[10]

After a chance meeting with a layman of great prominence in the YMCA, Wishard began to regard the upcoming International Convention of the YMCA at Louisville in 1877 as a tremendous opportunity for establishing an intercollegiate organization within the YMCA. With Wishard's guidance, the Princeton delegation sent out circulars to over two hundred colleges and normal schools, urging them to send representatives to the Convention from their Christian societies, if such existed. Twenty-five students did attend, and these collegiate representatives proceeded to supplement the activities of the general meetings with a special College Conference, where they discussed the function and the organization of their proposed Movement. The International Committee granted them wide latitude in these efforts, and made no attempt to influence their decisions or curtail their autonomy. After the students had arrived at a framework they considered suitable, they presented their suggestions to the larger assembly, which, by their approval, served to launch the Intercollegiate Young Men's Christian Association Movement.

Wishard, as head of the Princeton delegation which had called the College Conference and as Chairman of the College Conference, was a natural choice for service in one of the most significant developments of this new Movement, the office of Corresponding Secretary. Starting at the meager salary of $250 a year, and canceling other plans in order to answer this important calling, Wishard spared no pains in his efforts to consolidate and enlarge the intercollegiate fellowship through correspondence, and increasingly, visitation. As a result of this office, Wishard was in a better position than any other single person to shape and direct the nascent intercollegiate movement. It is therefore quite significant for our purposes to learn that Wishard had a profound dedication to the missionary cause — so profound, in fact, that he sought the counsel of several noteworthy clergymen before he decided that he should proceed with his work in the colleges rather than depart immediately for the mission field. A crucially important inspiration for Wishard's missionary concern was the example of Samuel Mills and the Society of the Brethren, whose story he heard for the first time at Union Seminary the winter following the conference at Louisville. From this moment on, Wishard made every effort to keep the cause of missions before the eyes of the Collegiate Associations, many of which, as converted Societies of missionary inquiry, already had a missionary emphasis."

Robert Wilder and the Princeton Foreign Missionary Society

About the same time as the Intercollegiate Movement was coming into being, Royal G. Wilder, the veteran missionary and member of the Brethren Society who had set sail for India more than thirty years earlier, returned to the United States on account of poor health, settling in Princeton where one of his older sons was about to enter college. Wilder soon founded the *Missionary Review*, which he continued to edit for the next decade. For the purposes of this account, however, the most significant aspect of his return was that he brought with him his twelve year old son, Robert Parmalee Wilder, who was to become in most every respect the founder of the Student

Volunteer Movement for Foreign Missions. As we will later show in detail, many of the ideas of the SVM can be traced to Robert Wilder, who was clearly indebted to his father and the original Brethren Society.

Robert P. Wilder entered Princeton College in the fall of 1881. He proved to be a brilliant student, as his later election to Phi Beta Kappa bears witness. His interests included Greek and philosophy, together with a special devotion to music. The excellence Wilder displayed in his studies was not purchased at the price of neglecting the Christian community at Princeton; much to the contrary, he was an active participant in the life of the church, serving as president and secretary of the Philadelphian Society, helping with Sunday School at the First Presbyterian Church in Princeton, and working as an officer in the prohibition society which successfully campaigned to close every saloon in the Princeton borough.[12]

In his junior year Wilder was invited to attend a conference of the Inter-Seminary Missionary Alliance (ISMA), meeting at Hartford, Connecticut in 1883. The ISMA had been formed in 1879, largely through the efforts of a friend of Luther Wishard's, the Princeton theological student Robert Mateer; and although technically it was composed of seminary students, Wilder and two other undergraduates from Princeton were invited because of their known missionary interest. The meeting proved a great inspiration to Wilder and his classmates. After a particularly moving address by Rev. A.J. Gordon of Boston, in which the speaker admitted that he had spent twenty years in the ministry before allowing himself to be fully empowered by the Holy Spirit, Wilder asked whether he, too, would need to wait twenty years before God could use him to the fullest.

"God is ready to give you the power of His Spirit," replied the older man, "as soon as you are ready to obey Him."[13]

Fired by the conference, the undergraduate delegates returned to Princeton with aspirations of effecting both a general revival and an awakening of mission interest on campus. In the interests of this latter objective, they founded that autumn the Princeton Foreign Missionary Society (PFMS), whose constitution read in part, "The object of this Society shall be the cultivation of a missionary spirit among the students of the College, the information of its members in all subjects of missionary interest, and especially the leading of men to consecrate themselves to foreign missions work . . . Any student of the College who is a professing Christian may become a member by subscribing to the following covenant: *We, the undersigned, declare ourselves willing and desirous, God permitting, to go to the unevangelized portions of the world.*" The Society also adopted a watchword: "The Evangelization of the World in This Generation."[14] Although membership was limited to those taking the pledge, the society's meetings were open to any student of the College seriously considering mission work as a life work. These were held in the home of Robert Wilder's father, and frequently the retired missionary would contribute to the evening's program, presenting insights gleaned from his experience and study. In another room of the house, Robert's older sister Grace supported the meetings with her prayers.

In retrospect, it is apparent that the Princeton Foreign Missionary Society was in fact the original cell of the extensive structure later to be known as the Student Volunteer Movement. As we will see when we study the SVM, not a single major characteristic of this latter organization was lacking from the PFMS. For the moment, however, let us direct our attention to a student missionary awakening in Great Britain, which was precipitated by an American and which would soon, by example and outreach, have an important impact on American students.

The Cambridge Missionary Seven

Dwight Lyman Moody (1837-1899) appeared an unlikely candidate to effect a religious revival among the elite student body of the ancient and distinguished Universities of Cambridge and Oxford. When Moody was four, his father, a Connecticut Valley farmer, died, leaving the care of nine children to his poverty stricken widow. Handicapped by his rural background and deprived of an adequate education, Dwight Moody spoke so poorly as a young man that the elders at his church discouraged him from participating in the prayer meetings. Nevertheless, Moody soon developed an effective manner of expressing himself which helped to transcend the limitations of his underprivileged background. After a brief but successful career as a businessman, Moody became active in the Chicago YMCA, as its President and General Secretary. Working through the YMCA, he helped to minister to the soldiers of the Union Army during the Civil War, organizing several hundred meetings for the Army YMCA which bordered Camp Douglas. Having thus established himself as an evangelist, Moody found it necessary to resign his YMCA position in 1871 in order properly to fulfill the demands of his work in public evangelism.[15]

Despite a number of remarkably successful evangelistic tours, including one to England in 1873, Moody, ever aware of his educationally deficient background, was hesitant to accept when in 1883 he received from students at Oxford and Cambridge an invitation to conduct a religious mission to these universities. His misgivings notwithstanding, Moody consented and then persisted in the face of an audience reception which was initially cold and disruptive. Soon, however, at both Oxford and Cambridge, students began to attend in increasing numbers and with increasing seriousness, until by the last meeting at Cambrige over 1800 students were present and listening attentively. Two of the Cambridge students converted by these meetings were C.T. Studd and Stanley Smith, both prominent University athletes. These two men joined with five other student athletes to form the "Cambridge Missionary Seven," a group of student athletes who had decided, largely on the impetus of Moody's meetings, to go to China as missionaries. Members of the Cambridge Seven sent out a deputation from among themselves to explain their missionary convictions to students in other British colleges and universities, and the story they communicated was a great inspiration to many.

Setting the Stage for Mount Hermon

Luther Wishard and his new assistant, a recent graduate of Williams College named Charles Ober, first heard the story of the Cambridge Missionary Seven from the brother of C.T. Studd, two years after Moody's Cambridge meetings. J.E.K. Studd, though not himself a member of the Cambridge Seven, was the captain of the university cricket team and had acted as chairman during Moody's Cambridge meetings. Like Wishard and Ober, he was attending a conference for Christian workers which Moody held annually at his conference grounds in Northfield, Massachusetts. After hearing of the success in Britain, Wishard and Ober coveted the prospect of a similar missionary awakening among American students, and with Moody's help, convinced Studd to alter his plans so that he might tour American colleges, telling the story of the Cambridge Missionary Seven. Studd spent over three months at this project, speaking at several intercollegiate conferences as well as twenty different colleges. One important reason why Studd's trip is remembered is because of the impact it had in redirecting the life of a young Cornell sophomore, a man whose work over the next sixty years was to be honored by the Nobel Peace Prize in 1946.

Though in most every external aspect the life of John R. Mott seemed to be that of a typical religious youth, Mott's plans and ambitions were in fact resting on an internal religious conflict, as he related in his later life. The talented and practical-minded Mott had great ambitions for a successful career in business or public life; and he felt somehow uneasy in the pervasive religious atmosphere of Upper Iowa University, which he attended during his freshman year. Mott felt threatened because the claims of Christianity on his life and his work conflicted with his personal plans. "Let it be repeated," he later wrote, "there are two views of one's life. One is that a man's life is his own, to do with as he pleases; the other that it belongs to another, and, in the case of the Christian, that the other to whom it belongs is Christ himself. At first, although I bore the name of Christian, I held the former or selfish view."[17] In an effort to work his way free of religious entanglements, Mott had transferred to Cornell, which was reputed at the time to be a "godless institution." But to his surprise, Mott was greeted upon arrival by a representative of the Cornell YMCA, and the friendship and assistance thus offered defeated Mott in his efforts to work free of religious entanglements. This encounter, moreover, revivified the conflict he had unsuccessfully tried to run away from, for it brought Mott to realize that his discomfort was internal and had to be resolved accordingly.

When J.E.K. Studd came to speak at Cornell that November, Mott was still reluctant to expose himself to any influence which might upset his own plans for his life. Nevertheless, this famous English athlete was a powerful drawing card, and after some hesitation, Mott tardily entered the lecture room to hear Studd quoting, "Young man, seekest thou great things for thyself? Seek them not! Seek ye first the kingdom of God." These passages stuck like barbs in his mind, and his conflict worsened to the point where it became the focus of all his thoughts and he was unable to sleep. The following morning he spent in restless solitude among the breathtaking gorges which bejewel the Cornell campus; by 2:30 that afternoon he had mustered up enough courage to obtain an interview with Studd. Studd encouraged Mott to ignore dogmatic assertions, but rather to investigate first-hand the original source material of Christian doctrine and belief, the New Testament. This meeting was, according to Mott's biographer, "the decisive hour of Mott's life."[18] He met with Studd several more times during the latter's week-long visit, and the two acquired a mutual admiration. The influence of Studd and of the students in the Cornell YMCA began to redirect the ambitions of the twenty-year old Mott, and he soon became actively involved in a prison ministry. Within a month of Studd's visit he was vice-president of the Cornell YMCA, and as a result of some careful study and thought over the Christmas recess, Mott decisively subjugated his will to that of his Lord. Thus evolved the commitment of a man who was to become perhaps the most remarkable missionary statesman in recent memory, who served among other capacities as the Chairman for over thirty years of the Student Volunteer Movement.[19]

Studd's tour was not the only fruit of this 1885 summer meeting at Northfield; for at this same meeting, the idea of a summer conference for students first crystallized in Wishard's mind.[20] Moody had made a suggestion that the buildings which were just being constructed for a boys' school at nearby Mount Hermon could be used to hold a Bible study conference for the general secretaries of the YMCA, at which he offered to preside. Wishard thought this was a marvelous idea, but for students rather than secretaries. As early as 1882, Wishard had been advocating that a separate conference be held for student representatives of the Intercollegiate YMCA Movement. Up to this point, the IYMCAM meetings had existed as sideshows to the quadrennial International Conventions held for the YMCA as a whole. For Mount Hermon, Wishard envisioned a kind of intercollegiate Bible study, which could serve as both a mechanism for training students in developing and communicating their faith, and as a forum for discussing the problems and the possibilities of the Intercollegiate Movement. Although Wishard then felt he lacked the authority to approach Moody on the possibility of leading such a conference, he sounded out his superiors on the matter, and the following April presented his ideas to the evangelist. Moody, however, had serious reservations. The first obstacle was Moody's reticence about speaking to students, still present despite his successes at the British Universities. Furthermore, Moody objected, college students are busy people, and are not likely to be able to set aside a month in the middle of the summer to study, of all things, the Bible. What if only a few students signed up? Nevertheless, Wishard persisted, and in April of 1886 Moody somewhat reluctantly admitted, "Well, I guess we'd better try it."

The student summer school was scheduled for the month of July, 1886, and the college secretary and his assistant, desperately short of time, set out immediately among the colleges to enlist delegates. At Cornell University Charles Ober located the young sophomore with whom Studd had been greatly impressed. As an officer of the YMCA, John Mott had already read with great interest the circular describing the conference, and was ready to part with his brand new set of Encyclopedia Britannicas, if necessary, to defray the cost of a summer with Moody. Ober and Mott then cooperated to round up a total of ten Cornell delegates. Among Luther Wishard's stops was his alma mater, Princeton College, where Robert Wilder was just completing his senior year. Wilder was hesitant to accept Wishard's invitation. He thought it would be better that his place be given to a student who had not yet graduated, so that any benefit from the conference might be brought back to the college. Wishard, however, was aware of Wilder's leadership among the mission-minded students of Princeton College, and he successfully persuaded Wilder, together with nine other students from the College, to attend. No single action could have had a greater impact on the course of the Mount Hermon Conference.

The Mount Hermon Conference, 1886

The Mount Hermon Conference began on July 6, 1886. Through the efforts of Wishard and Ober, two hundred and fifty-one students from eighty-six colleges had come together from all parts of the country to spend the month of July in the New England countryside. The conference was loosely organized with no set program or schedule. A month in duration, it adopted a casual atmosphere and a leisurely pace, with many meetings held out under the trees. Moody's emphasis was on training the students in personal evangelism, and he did not aggressively advocate foreign missions, nor was he particularly knowledgeable on the subject. Preaching and singing were given key roles in the presentations, because Moody regarded these as the two most effective means to communicate the gospel. Each morning he would give a Bible study, and students were invited to interrupt with their questions. No formal missionary emphasis was announced or planned, but this was largely because the conference lacked any formal structure. In a tentative schedule arranged by Wishard and Ober, a large place had been given to missionary themes.[21] Nevertheless, the impetus for a mission movement came from the students, and was not organized or promoted from the older generation.

Several students, in fact, had come to Mount Hermon independently with specific missionary interest. At both Cornell and Princeton, groups of students had prepared for the conference with explicit prayer for the consecration of many men to mission work. A man from Oberlin and a man from Harvard had also conceived of Mount Hermon as an opportunity for a commitment of young men to missions. These separate groups were not, however, aware of their common interest until Robert Wilder sent out a notice for all interested in missions to meet. Soon, a core of twenty-one mission-minded students developed, who if they had not already done so, subscribed to the pledge which Robert Wilder had brought with him from the PFMS. Through the personal work of this group, mission interest began to spread rapidly among the members of the conference. John Mott recalls his first meeting with Robert Wilder: "The first time I heard about missions down there [was] half-way to the river [when] a fellow began to talk to me on German philosophy, in which he had heard I was interested. Before long he wove in the subject of missions. I evaded it. He tactfully held me to it. That was Robert Wilder."[22]

As the number of students taking the volunteer pledge began to increase, Wilder and others started searching for a way to present the mission cause to the conference as a whole. They approached Dr. A.T. Pierson, a leading authority and great advocate of missions, with the request for a missionary address. "Well," he replied unknowingly, "I don't suppose that will be a popular subject here."[23] Nevertheless, the students persuaded him to speak, and on the Friday evening of July 16 Dr. Pierson spoke to a packed auditorium which included almost every delegate, presenting his message that "all should go, and go to all." This sermon helped prepare the soil for the missionary commitments yet to come, as it set many of the men thinking about their obligations to the unreached. The stress on the universality of both the mission call and the mission field was to become one of the key characteristics of the SVM.

Eager to keep the topic of missions before the delegates, Robert Wilder soon requested Moody's permission to hold a presentation in which ten students would address the convention on the subject. Moody was unacquainted with Wilder, so he consulted Wishard and Ober, who naturally gave their full approval. Three sons of missionary parents and seven nationals were hastily gathered from among the delegates, and on the Friday evening of July 23, the students assembled for the so-called "Meeting of Ten Nations," a gathering which Mott believes "did more to influence decisions than anything else which happened in those memorable days."[24] Students representing each of ten different nations presented the spiritual needs of their country in a three minute address, each one closing with the words "God is Love," spoken in the tongue of their people. The effect was tremendous. Wilder recalls: "Seldom have I seen an audience under the sway of God's spirit as it was that night."[25] A visiting missionary concluded the presentation with the challenge, "Show, if you can, why you should not obey the last command of Jesus Christ."[26] John Mott was among those affected by the meeting, and he proceeded to spend more than one night in prayer doing "conclusive thinking," afterwards adding his name to the growing list beneath the Princeton declaration.

The next missionary address was delivered by Dr. William Ashmore, a missionary from China who had heard about the Mount Hermon Conference while passing through the New England area on furlough. He had immediately cancelled all his engagements for over a week in order that he might press upon the students the claims of China, feeling that Mount Hermon was possibly "the best recruiting ground I can find."[27] On Tuesday morning, July 27, Dr. Ashmore encouraged the delegates to "look no longer upon missions as a mere wrecking expedition, but as a war of conquest." Many were stirred by his address. At this time the number of students signing the Declaration had risen to about fifty and the atmosphere of the conference was acquiring a pervasive missionary flavor. Whether the men were swimming, running, eating, or just taking a walk in the woods, the favorite topic of discussion was missions. As the number of volunteers increased, it became increasingly difficult for any delegate to get through the day without confronting the claims of the mission field. Most of the decisions to accept this call, however, were apparently made in private, the fruit of time spent in prayer and reflection.

On Friday, July 30, a meeting of volunteers was held in Crossley Hall from twilight to midnight. One by one, the men stood up and explained the reasons for their self-consecration to the mission effort. The power of this meeting was remembered by many for the rest of their lives. During these last days of the conference, the number of volunteers increased more rapidly than ever before, the climax not being reached until the morning after the conference ended, when a farewell meeting of prayer was held for those who had signed the Princeton declaration. There were by that time ninety-nine student volunteers. As these ninety-nine students knelt in prayer, one final man opened the door and slipped in, filling the ranks of what was to be known as the "Mount Hermon One Hundred." Almost forty percent, therefore, of the two hundred and fifty-one students meeting at Mount Hermon committed themselves to mission service, a remarkable result in view of the fact that not a single mention of missions was made in the circular Wishard provided to advertise the Conference. Although some of these men were detained from the mission field, a large number spent the majority of their lives in service overseas.

Growth and Expansion

Three or four days before the close of the Conference, Charles Ober, Wishard's associate, had suggested to some of the students during a tramp through the countryside that a deputation of students be sent among the colleges of North America, even as the Cambridge Missionary Seven had recently sent a deputation throughout England, with great success.[28] By making students aware of the mission uprising at Mount Hermon, it was hoped that additional young men and women would ally themselves with the mission cause. Ober's proposal was presented to all the volunteers when they next assembled as a group, and they greeted the plan with hearty approval, choosing Wilder, Mott, and two men from Yale and De Pauw to represent them during the following school year. A layman from New York City offered to provide the financial support necessary for such a tour; and Wishard and Ober, as officers of the YMCA, volunteered to book their speaking engagements at the college chapters.

Problems soon arose, however. Of the four men chosen, only Wilder was not then in the midst of a college course. The others were also needed by the Christian Associations in their colleges. Both church leaders and college advisors counseled these three young men against interrupting their college career with such an undertaking;[29] and one by one, they wrote to announce that they would be unable to follow through as members of the deputation. Wilder was deeply disappointed. Wishard feared the consequences this apparent cooling might have on the One Hundred, finding it "utterly impossible to comprehend and sympathize with the 'reasons', the 'obstacles', the 'difficulties' which the fellows present."[30] Wilder, however, chose to leave the matter between them and the Lord. "Mott's, Riley's and Taylor's action may be of God," he wrote in a letter at the time. "We may have relied too much on *numbers* and too little on *God*. God might just as well use strong things but He uses *weak* things instead 'That no flesh should glory in his presence.' "[31]

Unfortunately, numerous roadblocks were now converging to impede Wilder's progress as well. For many years he had suffered from poor health; poor enough, in fact, that he had been forced to stop out of college in his junior year in order to regain his strength. Travelling and speaking could be a gruelling, strenuous undertaking, and no companions remained to help shoulder the burden. Robert Wilder's father was in very poor health, and the doctors were giving him but six months to live. It seemed likely that were Robert to leave, he would never see his father again, and both father and son were understandably very reluctant to see Robert leave under such circumstances. Furthermore, the elder Wilder was counting on his son's assistance with the editorial work for *The Missionary Review*. A year spent on the campuses would mean an extra year before completing graduate training at Union Theological Seminary and would introduce a corresponding delay into the time by which Robert could either be fully useful to the *Missionary Review* or sail for the mission field. And although Robert's sister Grace encouraged and supported him fully, some members of the Wilder family expressed their judgment that Robert's plan to join this "band of Missionary Troubadours is one of doubtful utility and propriety."[32] But if Wilder did not go, if nobody went, the future of this student uprising would be in extreme jeopardy. Despite all these obstacles, therefore, Robert Wilder remained of the conviction that even if it was necessary to go alone, it was the Lord's will that he spend the next year telling other students about the Mount Hermon One Hundred. His father's approval was slow in coming. For two days the former missionary said nothing. Then he called Robert into his study and said, "Son, let the dead bury their dead. Go thou and preach the kingdom."[33]

Although Wilder had reconciled himself to making the trip alone, consultation and prayer soon convinced him of the wisdom of seeking a companion. He chose to contact John N. Forman, also the son of missionary parents to India, and a member of the original Princeton group, though not a Mount Hermon delegate. After a night of thoughtful prayer, Forman agreed to postpone graduate work at Union Theological Seminary so that he might accompany Wilder on the deputation.

Wilder and Forman began their tour in Maine, soon after the commencement of the 1886-87 school year. Wilder's health immediately created serious problems, for at Bowdoin, the strain of too many meetings and interviews was more than he could endure, and he "collapsed completely."[34] Upon seeing the doctor, he was warned that to continue the tour meant running the risk of a permanent breakdown. Nevertheless, after taking the matter to the Lord, Forman and Wilder felt that "the success of the movement was worth the price of risking one person's breakdown,"[35] and so, after a brief respite, they pushed on. Usually they travelled together, although they sometimes separated so as to reach more institutions. Wilder's determination in embarking on and continuing the tour, in the face of overwhelming obstacles, reflects his convictions about the importance of the movement even at this early stage. So important to Wilder was the momentum of Mount Hermon that he was willing to delay his career and even jeopardize his health in order to ensure its preservation. His belief in the importance of the movement was in turn based on a rock-hard conviction about the eternal importance of the mission enterprise. Only such a conviction could result in such motivation.

The phenomenal results of his tour with Forman are somewhat more comprehensible in the context of this powerful drive. Forman and Wilder visited over one hundred and sixty-two institutions in a period of eight months, and secured the names of over two thousand volunteers, each of whom signed the same declaration as members of the original Mount Hermon One Hundred. What was soon to be called the Student Volunteer Movement was now firmly established on an extensive intercollegiate basis. Although the Mount Hermon Conference had been composed entirely of men, since attendance was limited to members of the Young Men's Christian Association, over five hundred women were enlisted as a result of these first efforts to extend the movement. Far fewer women than men attended college in the late nineteenth century, so this number implies more than adequate representation.

Credit for the success of the tour must be given not only to the heroic perseverance of Wilder and the partnership of Forman, but also to the Mount Hermon delegates who, in anticipation of such a harvest, had returned to their schools and planted the seeds of mission commitment. The number of new volunteers probably also reflected the impact of Studd's 1885-1886 tour, as well as the steady efforts of Wishard for at least seven years. Wilder and Forman, however, significantly deepened and broadened the already substantial base of affected colleges.

The following summer brought as an encore performance the second Student Summer School, this time held at nearby Northfield, Massachusetts. Moody again presided, and the focus was again on the study of Biblical truths and how to convey them to others. Mount Hermon, 1886, was in fact the beginning of a tradition, and "Northfield Conferences" were held annually for many years. There was never any effort to impose a missionary slant from the above, however; any missionary impulse was allowed to arise spontaneously from the students themselves. Among the delegates to the Northfield Conferences were students from Great Britain, and their contact with American students resulted in a cross-fertilization of ideas and methods which proved profitable to both countries.

During the 1887-1888 school year, the second school year to follow the Mount Hermon conference, the still unorganized movement was left entirely without supervision or guidance. After John Forman departed for India, Robert Wilder was left alone in the leadership of the movement, which responsibility he had to share with the demands of his school work at Union Theological Seminary. (A fellow seminarian helped out by handling the correspondence for the Movement, storing the records in boxes beneath his bed.) At the same time, the fresh enthusiasm of the newly enlisted volunteers continued to provide the movement with momentum, and the number of recruits climbed over the 3000 mark. Like a speeding car without a driver, the movement was in an extremely critical and precarious state. Perceptive observers could begin to pinpoint several dangerous tendencies.

These problems can be delineated as follows.[36] First, the volunteer bands in different colleges were beginning to acquire different characteristics: their stated purposes, their methods of working, and their constitutions were often quite dissimilar. Much of the power of the movement, by contrast, was derived from its unity, established initially by the common acceptance by all volunteers of the same volunteer pledge. If the organizational bodies through which the volunteer movement carried out its collegiate existence came to institutionalize a disunity, much of this power would be irretrievably lost. The need to rectify this situation was an urgent one, for with the passing of time the individual organizations would lose their malleability. Time was also beginning to see the decline of the movement in some colleges, and this was a second area of concern. Without an organized effort to stimulate and revitalize the widely scattered bands of volunteers, many would inevitably grow cold. Finally, a new group of mission-minded students would occasionally find itself in competition or conflict with existing agencies.

These problems provided the grounds for discussion mong fifty student volunteers who had gathered at the 1888 Northfield Conference. The desire to extend the movement was also in their thoughts, as it had not yet reached about four-fifths of the institutions of higher learning on the continent,[37] though firmly established in some of the largest and best. Charles Ober again provided invaluable counsel, suggesting a scheme of organization which met with wide approval. It was based on the observation that the student missionary uprising was intimately connected with the Intercollegiate YMCA Movement: it had come into being during the Mount Hermon Conference, a function of the Intercollegiate Movement; much of its extension was due to Wilder and Forman's tour of student YMCA and YWCA chapters; and, predictably, most of its members were part of either the YMCA or the YWCA, or, in the seminaries, the Inter-Seminary Missionary Alliance. By tying the free-floating bands to the Christian Associations in the colleges, and to the ISMA in the seminaries, the movement would automatically inherit an organizational structure of great utility for its establishment, maintenance, and extension. The volunteers assembled at the 1888 Northfield Conference were convinced of the advantages; and soon forthcoming was a formally organized entity with the predictable appelative, the

"Student Volunteer Movement for Foreign Missions." Its executive committee would consist of representatives chosen by each of the three organizations listed above, and the localized volunteer bands would effectively constitute the missionary departments of the Christian Associations and the ISMA. This plan was soon approved by the organizations concerned, and representatives for the SVM's executive committee were chosen as follows: John R. Mott for the YMCA, Nettie Dunn for the YWCA, and Robert P. Wilder for the ISMA (and its Canadian counterpart).[38]

So effective was this approach in averting the perils of the movement's early stage, that in 1891 Robert Wilder could extend judgment that the organization "seems to be nearly perfect. By uniting our Movement with the three leading student organizations . . . we have given it permanency and patronage and a limitless field in which to expand."[39] John Mott has suggested that "had the counsels of some prevailed [at the time of the Northfield meeting] . . . in all human probability the Movement would have disintegrated."[40] The missionary uprising had brilliantly maneuvered its untested bark through perilous shoals on which it might easily have foundered; and now found itself in open waters, its sails puffed by a steady and reliable tailwind. This does not imply, of course, that its sails were in perfect trim, nor that its course was completely true. Some mission experts have maintained that the dependence of the executive committee on the selection of its members by these other organizations was, much later, to deflect the vessel's compass like a local disturbance in the earth's magnetic field, driving the Movement onto a faulty course which, over time, was to spell its demise. They have suggested that the Movement would have fared better with a self-perpetuating executive committee, or perhaps a committee elected from the volunteer bands.[41] The events of the early period of the Movement, however, can do little to resolve this debate, since its early leaders perceived themselves as functionally independent, and acted accordingly.

A further result of the 1888 Northfield Conference was the decision to ask Robert Wilder to forego his educational plans for the next year in order that he might once again visit the college campuses. Wilder's primary task was to reorganize the volunteer groups into branches of the YMCA, in accordance with the constitution of the newly formed SVM. He successfully achieved this goal, for within a couple of years, all of the Volunteer Bands were safely within the fold of one of the larger organizations. In the course of this tour, he visited almost one hundred institutions, a quarter of which had been touched previously and enlisted 600 new Volunteers. The following year, Wilder's position as travelling secretary was filled by a remarkable graduate of Princeton's 1889 class, Robert E. Speer. During his senior year Speer had been the president of the Philadelphian Society, the managing editor of the *Princetonian,* and member of the Princeton football team.[42] He is remembered daily by scholars using the Robert E. Speer Library at Princeton Seminary. During his missionary tour to the campuses, Speer gathered a remarkable 1100 new volunteers from 110 institutions.

The 1890-1891 school year, the fourth to follow the Mount Hermon Conference, was a very special year in the Movement's history; for the Movement's first International Convention was held from February 26 to March 1, 1891. Almost 600 volunteers from 159 institutions, representing the whole of North America east of the Rockies, flocked to Cleveland, Ohio, chosen because of its geographical centrality with respect to the

colleges of the United States and Canada. The
Convention helped to establish the legitimacy of the
Movement in the eyes of the Church, and helped secure
the approval of mission agencies and other Christian
organizations, whose representatives observed the
proceedings. Meeting from Thursday evening to Sunday
evening, the Convention covered a wide range of topics,
including the history and platform of the Student
Volunteer Movement; preparation necessary for a
mission career; procedures for applying to the mission
boards; varieties of foreign missionary service; and the
needs of specific geographical regions, cultural groups,
and religious groups. The evening sessions were often
less technical or practical than the morning and
afternoon sessions, and more inspirational in emphasis.
The proceedings of the convention were printed and
made available for those who were unable to attend, as
well as for the church in general. The Cleveland
Convention set a precedent; it foreshadowed a tradition.
For almost half a century, SVM Conventions were held
every four years, so that an opportunity might be
provided for each student generation to unite in its
concern for foreign missions.

With the Cleveland Convention of 1891, the Student
Volunteer Movement had come of age. Still bursting with
youthful vitality and idealism, the Movement had
achieved a certain maturity of form and expression, had
acquired a sturdy skeletal structure and a powerful
physique, and had presented itself to its elders as a
competent, independent and productive entity. We
therefore end our chronological narrative to discuss the
characteristics of the early Student Volunteer Movement.
In this discussion we will confine ourselves for the most
part to the Movement before the turn of the century,
since this was the era in which SVM was the affair

exclusively of students. (It was always, of course, exclusively the affair of volunteers, but time in its unassuming and inexorable manner gradually transformed volunteers of the younger generation into volunteers of the middle and older generation. Only the early movement was run by individuals uniformly on one side of the middle-age threshold.)

4

Some Characteristics of the Early Movement

Like people, movements may be explained and understood in terms of their characteristics. Although such an attempt may occasionally obscure the diversity and dynamics of the organism, individual or collective which it hopes to comprehend, it may nevertheless prove invaluable in reconstructing that entity's unique personality. This chapter, therefore, is devoted to just such an effort.

Spiritual Characteristics

Volunteers repeatedly emphasized their dependence on prayer, crediting prayer with an essential role in the success of the Movement and the mission enterprise as a whole. "The Student Volunteer Movement owes everything to prayer," according to John Mott. "It was conceived in days and nights of prayer at Mount Hermon. The missionary enthusiasm which it called forth all over the student field had its springs in prayer. Its secretaries were all chosen under the clear guidance of the Holy Spirit in answer to persevering prayer . . . It was in a series of three prayer meetings that the permanency of the Movement was ensured by effecting its wise organization."[1] Forty-five years later Mott still maintained that prayer provided "incomparably the most important source of the vital energy of the Movement."[2] "Prayer and missions are as inseparable as faith and works," he explained, "in fact, prayer and missions *are* faith and works."[3] The Movement's leaders perceived the objective of the Movement — the achievement of its watchword — as equally contingent upon a firm foundation of prayer. "The evangelization of the world in this generation depends first of all upon a revival of prayer . . . The condition and consequences of such prayers as this is a new outpouring of the Holy Spirit."[4]

Confidence in the power of the Holy Spirit was in fact a second key characteristic of the Movement's spiritual outlook. Dr. Gordon spoke frequently on the Holy Spirit and its importance for missions. Dr. Pierson explained the supernatural basis of missions at the 1891 Convention: "The promise of the Father is the enduement of the Holy Ghost."[5] Robert Wilder layed great emphasis on the Holy Spirit, challenging the delegates to "expect a Pentecost upon the foreign field."[6]

A final spiritual characteristic was confidence in the infallible guidance of the Holy Scriptures. The Great Commission, which inspired and directed the volunteer's missionary efforts, was derived from Scripture. Wilder listed Bible study as a prerequisite to the indwelling of the Holy Spirit.[7] The 1886 Mount Hermon Conference was designed primarily as a Bible study, and Mott considered, "the absolute faith in the authority of the Christian Scriptures and the Christ therein set forth"[8] as a key reason for the momentum which the Conference developed.

These three emphases — dependence on the infallible scriptures, on prayer, and on the power of the Holy Spirit — are equally reminiscent of recent evangelical and pentecostal movements, which also found their wellsprings within the student population.

Organizational Characteristics

The individual volunteer provided the atom, the elemental building block, for all of the larger structures within the organization of the SVM. A group of volunteers at a given institution who joined themselves together for instruction and fellowship created a Volunteer Band, the molecule for binding the individual atoms into a relationship of cooperation and support. Since all the members of the Band would be members of the Christian Associations in the colleges, (or the Inter-Seminary Missionary Alliance in the seminaries), the Band would effectively form the missionary branch of the larger campus group. Moreover, the Band would provide an official on-campus representative for the SVM.

The internal activities of the Band focused on the maintenance and augmentation of missionary interest and intelligence among its members.[9] To this end a collective study of mission fields, mission biographies, and mission policy was undertaken. Bands worked to make mission literature available for their use and that of others, frequently establishing and developing a campus library on missions. Externally, the Band took efforts to interest and educate fellow students in the topic of world missions, holding open meetings for general audiences. It was naturally a significant factor in the recruitment of fresh men for the Movement. As part of the Movement's policy of supporting rather than competing with established religious organizations, Bands actively participated in the neighboring churches, helping in the Sunday Schools and Christian Endeavor Societies. Several succeeded in persuading neighboring churches or even their own institutions to provide the financial support necessary for sending one of their members to the field. The Band made frequent efforts to establish and maintain a friendly and cooperative relationship with representatives from the mission boards.

To facilitate correspondence between the numerous scattered Volunteer Bands and the executive committee, an additional link was provided in the form of a Coordinating Member (or Committee when necessary), who was responsible for alternatively answering, compiling, or forwarding any information received from a given geographical region, usually a state.

As explained above, the Executive Committee was composed of representatives chosen by three dominant Christian organizations: the YMCA for men on college campuses, the YWCA for women on college campuses, and the ISMA for seminary students. A fourth organization, the Canadian counterpart of the ISMA, traditionally elected the same representative as the ISMA. The Executive Committee was charged with the task of overseeing the Movement as a whole; and in order to assist them in this responsibility they appointed several volunteers as secretaries. The travelling secretary followed in the tradition of Wilder and Speer, personally visiting educational institutions in order to consolidate and extend the Movement. As the Movement enlarged, the need developed for several such secretaries, and at times up to a half dozen would hold the position simultaneously. A corresponding secretary was responsible for keeping track of the volunteers, tabulating statistics, distributing printed matter, and managing the treasury. An editorial secretary was responsible for keeping the Movement before the church and the volunteers, and corresponded regularly with prominent periodicals. The SVM stocked a fairly extensive supply of missionary literature, and offered these books at a discount, primarily as a service to volunteers. Over one hundred titles were made available by 1891. They also produced a growing literature of their own.[10]

Cognizant of the wisdom of experience and eager to enlist the support of their elders, the volunteers built into their Movement an Advisory Committee, composed of a small number of representative clergy and lay mission advocates. Both Rev. A.J. Gordon, whose message at the 1883 Hartford Convention had helped inspire the formation of the PFMS, and Rev. A.T. Pierson, a leading authority on missions who had helped formulate the Movement's watchword, were early members of this committee. The Executive Committee promised to confer with the Advisory Committee before taking any important step in the development of the Movement.[11]

The SVM was emphatically not an agency for placing and supporting missionary personnel. Its position with respect to the mission boards was that of a recruiting office. It endeavored to provide increasing numbers of candidates better prepared and better qualified than those to which the boards were accustomed. Although it called for no new sending agencies, it did call for the rapid extension of existing agencies, frequently to the consternation of mission executives who feared an ensuing letdown. When a mission agency rejected a volunteer on grounds of insufficient funds, the SVM encouraged him to repetition after personally enlisting his own support.

A rapid turnover rate is evident in almost all of the positions created by the SVM's organizational apparatus. The officers were volunteers, often those of the deepest commitment, and all but a handful eventually reached the foreign field.[12] The notable exception to this rule is John Mott, who as chairman of the organization for over thirty years, provided it with leadership and administrative talent for a full generation. (Mott's long tenure, it might be added, complicates the task of isolating and analyzing the merits of the early organization's structure independent of Mott and his influence.

Unity and Universality

The criteria determining membership in the SVM were fundamentally different from those defining affiliation with the traditional Protestant form of ecclesiastical fellowship, namely, the denominational church. The volunteer's eligibility was a function of two factors: his educational status, and his willingness to make a sacrificial commitment. As a result, the Volunteer Movement drew a unified corps of young collegians, each having reached a similar plateau in his individual odyssey, each surveying with similar vision the landscape stretching out beneath his feet. The eligibility requirements, the organization into Volunteer Bands, and the consequent *esprit de corps*, all bear an important resemblance to the religious orders of the Catholic

Church. This form of fellowship has been given the name 'sodality', or brotherhood, to distinguish it from the 'modality' represented by the neighborhood church.[13] Factors influencing participation in the neighborhood church are, by contrast, often geographical or hereditary. One attends Middlebury Presbyterian Church because it is one of only three churches in Middlebury and because it is where one's parents attend. It represents an established enterprise, a pre-ordained structure, a modality; and its membership encompasses a vast range of different ages and social groupings.

Because of its differing structure, the Student Volunteer Movement did not need to compete with the established churches. Each volunteer could maintain his position within the denominational framework while committing his will to an objective which cut across denominational lines. The perpendicular bond thus created could actually help thread together the denominational strands, producing a sturdy fabric of sufficient integrity to clothe other peoples in the knowledge of Christ. The missionary impulse united the sympathies of Christians who retained differing conceptions of church government and doctrine, and the ecumenical fusion which resulted was a significant factor in promoting a strong and unified missionary front, crucial for both support at home and acceptance abroad. This spirit of unity was essential to the character of the Movement. It vigorously eschewed any parochialism or sectarianism, whether denominational or geographical. Its leaders introduced the Movement into nearly all areas of the United States and Canada, and tried successfully to stimulate the creation of similar movements in European and Scandinavian countries. Nor did parochialism infect their perception of the field: the field was the world.

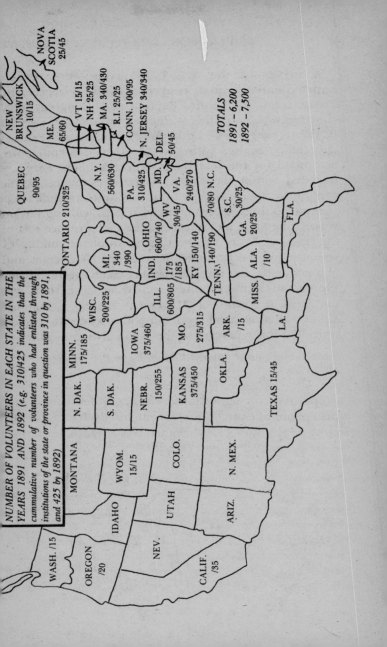

NUMBER OF VOLUNTEERS IN EACH STATE IN THE YEARS 1891 AND 1892 (e.g. 310/425 indicates that the cummulative number of volunteers who had enlisted through institutions of the state or province in question was 310 by 1891, and 425 by 1892)

TOTALS
1891 – 6,200
1892 – 7,500

NOVA SCOTIA 25/45

NEW BRUNSWICK 10/15

QUEBEC 90/95

ONTARIO 210/325

ME. 65/60

VT 15/15
NH 25/25
MA. 340/430
R.I. 25/25
CONN. 100/95
N. JERSEY 340/340
DEL. 50/45

N.Y. 560/630

PA. 310/425

MD. 240/270

VA. 240/270

WV 30/45

N.C. 70/80

S.C. 30/25

GA. 20/25

FLA.

OHIO 660/740

MI. 340/390

IND. 175/185

KY 150/140

TENN. 140/190

ALA. /10

MISS. /15

LA.

WISC. 200/225

ILL. 600/805

IOWA 375/460

MO. 275/315

ARK. /15

MINN. 175/185

N. DAK.

S. DAK.

NEBR. 150/255

KANSAS 375/450

OKLA.

TEXAS 15/45

MONTANA

WYOM. 15/15

COLO.

N. MEX.

IDAHO

UTAH

ARIZ.

WASH. /15

OREGON /20

NEV.

CALIF. /35

A survey of the first 6,000 volunteers reveals approximately equal representation between the Presbyterian, Methodist, Baptist, and Congregational churches, which together accounted for about 85 percent of the recruits.[14] The Lutheran, Episcopal, and Friends churches, together with several other denominations, accounted for the remaining sixth. (Catholics were not included within the ranks.) Careful estimates of the geographical distribution of the volunteers indicate a remarkably homogeneous membership, with significant representation in almost every state and province east of the Rockies. There was no disproportionate buildup of volunteers in the pathbreaking states of New Jersey and Massachusetts, according to statistics taken five years after the Mount Hermon Conference. In no sense, then, was the Student Volunteer Movement merely a regional affair. The Movement recruited both sexes, with women providing thirty percent of these initial volunteers.

Locations of Sailed Student Volunteers by Percentages

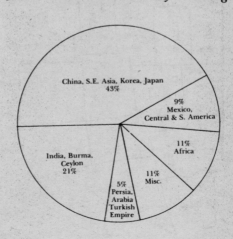

An evaluation of the 2,953 volunteers who sailed for the mission field in the first twenty years of the Movement reveals the following breakdown;[15] China, Southeast Asia, Korea, and Japan — 43%; India, Burma, and Ceylon — 21%; Africa — 11%; Mexico, Central and South America (largely papal) — 9%; Persia, Arabia, and the Turkish Empire — 5%; Miscellaneous — 11%. By 1920, volunteers from over sixty different Christian communions or denominations had sailed under the auspices of 66 different sending agencies.[16]

The early SVM reveals an almost official endorsement of the military metaphor. Overlooking each page of the printed copy of the 1894 Convention Proceedings are the words, "The World's Conquest"; and the 1898 Convention was conceived by its organizers as a "Council of War."[17] Volunteers, or "recruits," were often "enlisted." Even the watchword was reminiscent of military affairs, for as Robert Speer pointed out in 1898, military slogans are as old as *Carthago delenda est.*[18] Rev. Judson Smith explained the command structure at the 1894 convention: "Every missionary is a general, and must be thoroughly prepared for his post . . . The *captains* and the *soldiers of the line* must come from the native agency."[19] The notion of advancing in a common front, in order to achieve a common objective, obviously reflected an appeal to unity.

The Watchword

An expression of its comprehensive objective, 'The Evangelization of the World in This Generation' remained always the characteristic challenge of the Movement in America. "Not a few observant Christian leaders — regard this as the most distinctive, the most original, as well as the most daring contribution of the

Volunteer Movement."[20] The nature of the watchword's appeal has been analyzed above. Here we will study its history and discuss its contribution to the Movement.

Soon after the Europeans began to acquire a realistic knowledge of the locations and numbers of their fellow human beings, perceptive mission advocates, such as William Carey in the late eighteenth century, began to think in terms of world evangelization. Beginning at least as early as 1836, there are records of pastors, missionaries, or groups of missionaries proclaiming the possibility of world evangelization within their generation.[21] For some, once was not enough! In 1860 the zealous Earl of Shaftesbury announced to a mission conference that the church had sufficient means "to evangelize the globe fifty times over."[22] The fact that such a notion was conceivable indicates that the less ambitious proposal had by this time acquired some currency in mission circles.

Rev. A.T. Pierson of Detroit, who was probably the one to cast the watchword into its final form, was first charmed by this vision after reading the 1871 sermon of an English Baptist minister, which estimated that a wholehearted effort would see the world's evangelization in fifteen or twenty years.[23] In the early 1870's, Pierson adopted as his personal motto a phrase inspired by Acts 13:36: "To his own generation rendering service under the will of God."[24] Insofar as it is attributable to Pierson, the watchword appears to be a product of these two influences.

In late 1881, Pierson used the medium of R.G. Wilder's *Missionary Review* to publicly answer in a resounding affirmative the following query: "Can this World be Evangelized in Twenty Years?" (Twenty years was probably chosen as the time remaining in the century.)

The article was followed by a vigorous endorsement from the *Review's* editor, and Royal Wilder continued to urge this proposition on his readers, featuring, in three of the next four issues, articles on "Evangelizing the World in Twenty Years." Although the twenty year goal began to drop out of the picture, Royal Wilder was firmly committed to the idea of speedily evangelizing the world, as he reveals in an 1885 editorial: "The largeness of God's blessing on the puny efforts already made for evangelizing the heathen, demonstrate beyond the possibility of a doubt that we are well able to evangelize the *whole* world in a single generation."[25] His conviction undoubtedly had a tremendous impact on young Robert, so it is not surprising to find 'The Evangelization of the World in This Generation' as the watchword of the PFMS. Robert Wilder, the PFMS, and Pierson, all greatly influenced the Mount Hermon conference, so it is also as expected that the watchword played an influential role in the SVM's early stages. "At the Mount Hermon Conference." recalls Robert Wilder, "the words 'the evangelization of the world in this generation,' or their equivalent, were frequently used in personal work and public addresses, and were, undoubtedly, one of the principal causes which brought so many to volunteer."[26] The watchword was officially adopted in 1889, although it was used by the travelling secretaries from the Movement's inception.[27]

The point has already been made that the students considered the watchword as more than just an idealistic dream. Initially, at least, it was a living hope, an ambitious but concrete goal. What factors convinced these college students that *they* could accomplish a task which had eluded more than fifty previous generations of Christians? Certainly they expected God's direction and support in every aspect of the enterprise. "Let us never, never dare to leave for foreign service until endued with power on high,"[28] Wilder warned. But what was unique about this age? What stirred this unprecedented confidence? What factors were taken into account when calculating such an ambitious time scale? They were for the most part human factors and practical considerations. As we have seen, the wealth and manpower of the church, the opportunities made possible by improvements in transportation and communication, and all the trappings of the industrial age, were marshalled to support the feasibility of the enterprise. Robert Speer was convinced that even "if this were a human issue there would be no doubt of its possibility." "A hundred years ago it may not have been so, but what a contrast between that day and now!"[29] Practical considerations were interpreted as "signs of the times" revealing God's blessing on the missionary enterprise. Pierson listed world-wide exploration, communication, assimilation, civilization, emancipation, preparation, and organization as "seven great wonders, indicating to us that the fullness of time has come to evangelize the world in one generation."[30] Human factors were only considered, however, in light of God's promise of support. They were viewed in the context of precedents which, the volunteers believed, were illustrations of that support.[31] The most notable of these was the spread of the early church throughout the Roman Empire. Recent missionary successes were also illuminated as examples.

Volunteers calculated the number of missionaries necessary to achieve this task. "In a generation, one missionary from this land, if supplied with the necessary means and native helpers, could, without difficulty, have the gospel preached, and preached effectually, to every one of . . . 50,000 souls."[32] Convocations of missionaries to India and China suggested numbers of similar magnitude.[33] To reach one billion individuals then, 20,000 missionaries would be necessary. A mere one percent of the American college graduates anticipated in the following generation would be sufficient to fill this need.[34]

In 1936, Mott reminded the Indianapolis Convention that the watchword was never regarded "as a prophecy of what was likely to take place."[35] Emphasis was placed on what could and should be done, and the SVM never abandoned its conviction that the watchword represented both a possibility and an obligation. Nevertheless, the challenge of the watchword seems to have been most concrete to members of the early SVM. During this initial period, there was frequent mention of a definite number of years, usually thirty or thirty-three. In 1892, and writing on behalf of the volunteers in general, Mott even dared to state that the watchword's achievement was seen as "a probability."[36] Although this exhibits an unusual lack of caution, it also reflects a confidence which, judging from the spirit of the early writings, was anything but uncommon.

One did not need to be a volunteer to adopt the watchword as one's personal motto. The SVM encouraged Christian laymen, churches, and organizations to adopt the watchword as a guiding principle, and many non-volunteers did, among them the laymen drawn into the Laymen's Missionary Movement. The watchword fell under some criticism, however, from leaders who feared it would encourage a hasty and superficial presentation of the gospel. They questioned the substance of the enthusiasm it was stirring up, and pointed to linguistic and cultural barriers which could be overcome only by time and patience. Gustav Warneck of Germany, whom Mott acknowledged as the "greatest modern authority on foreign missions,"[37] advocated abandoning "the rhetorical phrase."[38]

Some definitional problems with the watchword can be highlighted by comparing it to a contemporary slogan which has recently been acquiring currency: "A Church for Every People by the Year 2000." The new slogan is certainly more precise than the old watchword, and its fulfillment is clearly much more accessible to measurement. But this precision has its disadvantages as well as its advantages. The most obvious disadvantage will be readily apparent to anyone asking himself whether the SVM would have still been growing in 1910 had its watchword been, "The Evangelization of the World by 1905." Another difficulty arises from the fact that the year 2000 contains little which can be seen as evoking moral responsibility. A non-ephemeral duty can never, by definition, be chained to a date. A sense of obligation must be brought to the challenge of this new slogan; unlike the SVM's watchword, duty cannot be read out of the slogan itself. And yet the dual character of the SVM's watchword — both obligation and challenge — created its own problems, as the following attempt by Mott to explain the words, "in this generation" serves well to illustrate: "What is the meaning of 'this generation?' As far as the activities and the direct influence of the individual volunteers are concerned, it means within his own lifetime. As far as the activities and the direct influence of the Volunteer Movement as a whole at any given time are concerned, it means within a given period commonly known as a generation from that time. It is of constant application to successive generations as long as the world remains unevangelized."[39] The general tone of this passage stresses the sense in which the watchword encompasses an obligation, and the introduction of a deadline seems artificial and forced. What significance, after all, can "the activities and direct influence" of the volunteer have for the world's evangelization outside of the context of the enterprise as a whole? And how meaningful can the phrase "in his own lifetime" be for an elderly person? Furthermore, how seriously can one take the challenge of a deadline which is guaranteed to remain 33 years away?

Mott remained always a staunch supporter of the watchword. He enumerated countless benefits: "The watchword . . . widens and enriches one's sympathies . . . It makes impossible national, racial, social and religious barriers . . . the watchword stimulates and strengthens one's faith. Faith cannot grow without exercise . . . The watchword gives men vision."[40] "Contrary to the impression of some, the watchword has promoted thoroughness." "The watchword has widely promoted unity and cooperation."[41] The fifty-nine year old Mott could "truthfully answer that next to the decision to take Christ as Leader and Lord of my life, the watchword has had more influence than all other ideals and objectives combined to widen my horizon and enlarge my conception of the kingdom of God."[42]

The Volunteer Declaration

Both Wilder and Mott have described the volunteer declaration as the keystone to the arch of the Student Volunteer Movement. "Without this solid, binding factor," Mott argued, "the Movement long ago would have crumbled."[43] What was the origin of the volunteer declaration, and how was it viewed by the Christian community?

Although the Mount Hermon One Hundred were separated from most of the Brethren by a gap of several decades, the pledge which they signed was directly inspired by the constitution of the original Brethren Society, and was actually composed by one of its members! In this constitution are found the words: "No person shall be admitted who is under any engagement of any kind which shall be incompatible with going on a mission to the heathen." "Each member shall . . . hold himself in readiness to go on a mission when and where duty may call."[44] These words suggested to Royal G. Wilder, father of Robert Wilder and a member of the Andover Brethren Society, the following pledge for the Princeton Foreign Missionary Society: "We, the undersigned, declare ourselves willing and desirous, God permitting, to go to the unevangelized portions of the world." The students of the PFMS heartily endorsed this pledge, and defined their membership accordingly. Robert Wilder then introduced at the Mount Hermon Conference the following pledge, which contained a seemingly minor modification of the final clause: "We are willing and desirous, God permitting, to become foreign missionaries."[45] The word "missionary" was probably intended to clarify the formerly unstated objective in going "to the unevangelized portions of the world." The collegiate tour of Wilder and Forman added 2000 more names to a pledge which differed from the one used at Mount Hermon only in that it had now been transcribed into the singular. Since the pledge served to define the body of individuals to be organized, it was automatically a part of the Movement organized in 1888.

The original wording of the pledge made room for a certain ambiguity of interpretation. The phrase 'I am willing and desirous' was sometimes taken as an indication of mere willingness, and not of intention. A person can be willing to do several things simultaneously, but he can only intend to do one of them. From the beginning, however, the pledge was designed to signal an exclusive commitment. Wilder vigilantly defended the original wording, arguing that the word *desire* represented a matter of the will and the heart, whereas the word *purpose,* the proposed replacement, represented a matter purely of the will.[46] The consensus, however, maintained that the pledge was overly susceptible to misinterpretation, and after extensive discussion, volunteers convening at the 1892 Northfield summer conference decided to change the wording to the following: "It is my purpose, if God permit, to become a foreign missionary."[47] Since the intention was merely to clarify a meaning which remained unchanged, those having signed the old pledge were not required to sign again with the new wording. Furthermore, the pledge was henceforth to be known as a "declaration," ostensibly because the meaning of the word "pledge" was incompatible with the clause, "if God permit." A significant part of the reason for this change, however, was probably that the milder word, "declaration," would be greeted with a warmer reception in the Christian and collegiate communities.

(Both Wilder's 1886 pledge and the declaration adopted in 1892 contain the phrase "foreign missionary," whose meaning was destined, in the course of time, to become more general than the early volunteers would have wished. During the early 20th century, the words "foreign missionary" sometimes came to mean "church worker in a foreign country" with little or no evangelistic implications. Furthermore, as the frontiers of tomorrow must push beyond the frontiers of today, merely going to a "foreign" country came to entail, in many cases, considerably less than the pioneer scope which was implied by the original 1883 phrase, "to go to the unevangelized portions of the world.")

Many volunteers bore witness to the pivotal significance the declaration had in directing their life work. More than sixty years after providing his signature, George Sherwood Eddy recalled, "There have been a few crucial moments that have shaped my whole later life. One was the quiet evening, in 1893, in Union Theological Seminary when I signed the Student Volunteer declaration card ... At that moment I *became* a missionary."[48] Volunteers emphasized the binding effect of the declaration, and the *esprit de corps* to which it gave rise. Nevertheless, the declaration met with considerable criticism. Some felt that the declaration was unnecessary; others objected to the way in which it was used, or tended to be misused. They feared that many missionary commitments were being made for the wrong reasons; that they were the products, not of prayer and reflection, but of rhetoric.

A fundamental criticism of the entire Movement underlay this objection. Many Christians believed that the decision to become a foreign missionary should only be made in conjunction with the clear conviction that this was God's special will for one's life. Some observers felt the rhetorical effect of the watchword and the pressure for a commitment tended to push the student onto either the wrong path, or onto a path which God had not yet seen fit to illuminate for him. A clergyman from the Baptist mission board cautioned, "The only point in which I have any fear about this student Movement is that we shall forget that God only can call a minister, God only can make a missionary."[49] D.L. Moody himself, in fact, never approved the volunteer declaration for exactly this reason. "He maintained that it was a dangerous thing, especially in so important a field as foreign missionary labors, to overurge any individual to pledge himself. It was Moody's conviction that since the kingdom of God is comprehensive of all peoples, everywhere, the scene of a man's life work matters little; what is essential is for a man to be in the will of God, the place and manner of service will then be made through His guidance."[50] Warneck's reservations reflected this same concern: "It is hoped that this movement, otherwise so gladdening, will become increasingly sound and healthy by avoiding all wholesale driving."[51]

The Movement answered these objections by emphasizing their stipulation that the "declaration should be used only under the manifest guidance of the Spirit."[52] In fact, a major reason for the organization of the Movement was the need of having some means to regulate the declaration's use. Even when the declaration was used according to prescription, however, it was supported by a philosophy wherein each individual was held accountable to the missionary call. For those who disagreed, no general appeal to subscribe to the declaration could be considered a proper use.

The declaration, as well as the watchword and the entire SVM appeal, had an aura of urgency about it. It encouraged students to make a commitment *now,* and to start preparing for the mission field *now.* Many feared that if this sense of urgency became excessive, the volunteer might be encouraged to sail before obtaining adequate preparation. W.H. Cossum, the Movement's travelling secretary for 1890-1891, did little to allay these fears when he addressed the Cleveland Convention on "Immediate Sailing: Its Advantages and How Secured."[53]

"Don't stay in this country theorizing," he pleaded, "when a hundred thousand heathens a day are dying without hope." His attitude was not typical of the Movement's leadership, however, which encouraged both haste and preparation. Most of the ministers and missionaries invited to address the volunteers emphasized the importance of preparation. Robert Wilder later stated, "I never regretted completing my course of study [at Union Theological Seminary] before going out as a missionary."[54] D.L. Moody had offered to guarantee his support for two years if he would leave immediately. It is impossible to determine from the written records of the period whether excessive, counterproductive haste was common among the rank and file. A full evaluation would have to consider in detail their work on the field.

5

The Early Movement's Development — A Discussion

Some of the general historical factors necessary for the Movement's development have already been discussed in the section dealing with the Movement's background. Many of the streams of missionary enthusiasm which flowed together at Mount Hermon found their source in the rains which drenched the spiritual landscape of Williams College in the early 1800s. Other streams were swelled by this downpour. At Mount Hermon these waters were merged and redirected into a well-organized and comprehensive matrix of waterways, provided by the YMCA, the YWCA, and the ISMA.

A closer look at specific developmental influences helps to explain many of the individual characteristics of the SVM discussed in the last chapter. More than of any other individual, the Movement bears the stamp of the veteran missionary Royal Gould Wilder, though he passed away several months before the Movement was organized. Many of the ideas of Robert Wilder, the Princeton Foreign Missionary Society, and the Student Volunteer Movement are taken directly from this man. The last chapter described Royal Wilder's impact on both the pledge and the watchword. By introducing the pledge, Royal Wilder also helped to reproduce in the SVM the fraternal structure of the Brethren Society, for in both organizations a signed commitment laid the foundation for a characteristic camaraderie and *esprit de corps*. Many of the elder Wilder's convictions were indistinguishable from those of the mature SVM, and unquestionably served to shape them. Robert Wilder recalls his father addressing the PFMS: " 'The question,' he would say, 'is not why *should* you go, but, if you are a true servant of Christ, why should you *not* go where the need is greater than in the homeland.' He also impressed upon us the duty of seeking to evangelize the world in *our* generation."[1]

The Wilder family was a close-knit team, so it is not surprising that Robert's beliefs were close to his father's. Robert Wilder was the last of five children in the family; his sister Grace was two years older than he was and second to the last. Robert and Grace were the only children remaining on the mission field with their parents until the family returned to the states; and there were no other Europeans, missionary or otherwise, in that area of India. At the age of ten, Robert made up his mind to become a foreign missionary. "It seemed to me that there was nothing else to do, since the need abroad was so much greater than in America."[2] Grace became the "inseparable companion" of Robert's childhood, and her missionary convictions were no less deep than those of her brother. After entering college in the states, she became the leader of the thirty-four signatory members of the Mt. Holyoke Missionary Association. Its declaration? "We hold ourselves willing and desirous to do the Lord's work wherever he may call us, even if it be in a foreign field." Since Grace Wilder graduated in 1883, these young women must have "volunteered" before the PFMS was even organized! The authorship of their pledge can be in little doubt. Any paternal influence Robert may have felt was probably amplified by his father's death, which may well have had the psychological impact of "passing on the torch." Soon after Royal Wilder passed away on October 10, 1887, Grace Wilder and her mother returned to India, as did Robert Wilder a few years later.

We see then that the pledge, the watchword, the organization of the volunteer band, and a great deal of the philosophy of the Student Volunteer Movement, were present in the PFMS more than two years before the Mount Hermon Conference. The Conference made intercollegiate a fellowship which had already developed in the home of a Brethren Society missionary. The function of Mount Hermon was to take the seed of this fully evolved species and disseminate it throughout the college campuses, where it rapidly took root and spread. The final flower was no hybrid, but a true copy of the original, and this fact bears witness to the influence of Robert Wilder in shaping the SVM.

How is the rapid growth and early success of the movement best understood? Sympathetic Christian observers will agree with the Movement's founders, who saw the hand of God behind its creation and forward movement. "It seems clear, Wilder believed, "that the source of the modern missionary uprising among students must have been in heaven."[3] This interpretation will see the dependence of the Movement on prayer, the power of the Holy Spirit, and the Holy Scriptures as its most profound source of strength. Nor does this point of view denigrate the importance of the considerations already illuminated, for these spiritual characteristics can be regarded as a deeper ground of causation than the shallower factors which can be fathomed by human wisdom. Because they operate on different levels, spiritual explanations can support those of an historical nature, rather than clash with them. For example, the organization of the Movement, at least in its broad outlines, was an important reason for the growth of the early Movement; John Mott emphasized that this organization was adopted only after careful prayer.[4]

Many "down-to-earth" considerations have already been discussed at length. The Movement clearly owes a great deal of its success to its well-developed and powerful appeal, presented in Chapter 2. Its unity, discussed in Chapter 4, created a common front and permitted an unambiguous objective. "One reason for the great impression created by the Movement was that it made a clear, definite appeal for one cause only."[5] Its universality allowed it to build its strength from all parts of North America, and to exercise that strength in all parts of the world. (Its use of military metaphor may reflect an undesirable contribution from the spirit of Manifest Destiny, but it is beyond the scope of the present work to analyze the extent of such a contribution.)

Clearly, the Movement is much indebted to the extraordinary young men it was fortunate to have on board from the very start. Robert Wilder, John Mott, and Robert Speer were all gifted with first-rate minds; each exhibited a rare fusion of scholastic excellence and community activism; and each was an effective public speaker in his own way. Moreover, their differing talents complemented each other beautifully. The zeal born of

Wilder's earnest convictions was essential for launching the vessel; once underway, the maritime savvy of Mott was needed to keep things ship-shape.

The mentality of the age was an important factor in helping to bring many into harmony with the Movement and its objective, for the challenge of the watchword could not fail but strike a responsive chord among college students tuned to the spirit of the progressive era. We have seen that much of the appeal of the watchword stemmed from the volunteers' conviction that it did indeed represent a possibility. In this respect, they shared with the secular community a belief that they could build on their parent's efforts and thereby succeed where their parents had failed. They were drawn to their task, at least in part, by this inherited faith that things *could* be made better, that there *was* such a thing as "progress." We have seen further that the advances confirming the volunteers' confidence were the products of scientific and technological progress, the identical wellsprings of the *secular* optimism of the age. Evidently, therefore, the volunteers not only adopted the world's mindset, but embraced it largely for the world's reasons as well. Theirs, however, was a progressivism with a twist. Unlike their worldly counterparts, they retained a belief in man's sinful nature and in the corruption thus introduced into any human endeavor. Consequently, they believed that no undertaking could achieve eternal worth without God's assistance, that such an effort would instead, like the tower of Babel, inevitably disintegrate with the passing of time. As a result, the volunteers relied heavily on God's support for the higher success of their undertaking; their confidence was mingled with a humble sense of dependence on the Almighty. And this is as it must have been. For the missionary impulse — the conviction that every man needed to be told of Christ's saving grace — was itself based on the realization of every man's ultimate insufficiency before God.

6

Epilogue

From 1891 until approximately 1910, the Student
Volunteer Movement experienced a period of steady
growth. Each four years saw a student gathering whose
attendance exceeded by about fifty percent the one
before; and the average number of student volunteers
reaching the mission field each year climbed from about
one hundred to over three hundred. During the next
decade, the years from 1910 to 1920, the SVM
maintained and even somewhat raised this level, as each
Convention continued to draw approximately five
thousand students; and each year saw an average of five
hundred new missionaries march from the volunteer
ranks to service in foreign lands. About three quarters of
the male and unmarried female missionaries going out
from North America during the period from about 1900
to 1920 had signed the volunteer pledge; and although

many students of predetermined missionary commitment undoubtedly latched on to the Movement as it acquired general recognition, investigations conducted by the SVM indicated that about "seventy-five percent of the volunteers assign the activities of the Movement as the principal or determining factor in their decision to become missionaries."[2] Combining these two figures, one can infer that, remarkably, the Student Volunteer Movement had a key role in securing the commitments of roughly one half of the missionaries leaving from North America in the first two decades of the twentieth century; and many other new missionaries were probably influenced by the Movement in either a secondary or indirect manner. The SVM achieved this influence despite limiting its operations to the college field.

During this period of great influence, the SVM aided in the inspiration and the creation of numerous other movements, which can here be but briefly described. On their separate journeys to India, John Forman and Robert Wilder each spent several months in the nations of Europe stimulating student interest in missions; and many European countries subsequently developed their own student volunteer movements. Luther Wishard and later John Mott, largely on the impulse of their profound missionary beliefs, travelled the world in order to assist students from many distant and diverse countries in the creation of their own Christian Associations. These newly established communities then merged with the student Christian Associations of the United States and the strong, indigenous, organizations of other countries, to form in 1895 the World's Student Christian Federation (WSCF), of which the SVM's John Mott was promptly named General Secretary. The SVM, with its spirit of international unity and cooperation, also helped lay the groundwork for the

World Missionary Conference at Edinburgh in 1910,[3] a gathering of great and fundamental importance to many 20th century developments. The development in the United States of the Laymen's Missionary Movement provided an influential association of Christian businessmen who supported the mission enterprise financially; and this organization was founded by a student volunteer whose creative impulse was sparked by the SVM's Nashville Convention early in 1906. The LMM's motto was the SVM's watchword, and many of its members had signed the volunteer pledge during their college days.[4]

Many individuals who began their Christian service in the SVM later attained positions of great responsibility within the church as a whole; and no less an authority than the late "dean of church historians," Kenneth Scott Latourette, bears witness to their impact: "It was through the Student Volunteer Movements in these various lands that a large proportion of the outstanding leaders in the world-wide spread of Protestant Christianity in the twentieth century were recruited."[5] This foremost historian of the church was at one time himself a travelling secretary for the movement. The Presbyterian Board of Foreign Missions was for forty-six years under the direction of student volunteer Robert E. Speer, who was asked to fill the top position while still a student at Princeton Seminary.[6] He also served as moderator for the Presbyterian Church (PCUSA) in 1927. Student volunteer John Mott went on to have a brilliant career as an international missionary statesman, chairing, among many other gatherings, the Conference at Edinburgh in 1910, and raising millions of dollars to support Christian projects. In 1946 he was the recipient of the Nobel Peace Prize, a fitting acknowledgment of his personal impact and achievement.

The history of the Student Volunteer Movement after about 1920 is, unhappily, one of gradual decline. The triumphant conviction and the near palpable excitement, so characteristic of those early conventions, seems almost completely subdued in the gatherings of the 1920s. With reference to the conventions, the *Missionary Herald* could in 1891 exult, "God has touched the hearts of young men and women, leading them to respond, 'We are ready to go. Send us!' ";[7] whereas in 1936 it could merely yawn "that many came back to the college campuses determined to live a better life and to do more thinking along international lines."[8] In 1921, over six hundred volunteers entered mission service; sixteen years later barely three dozen. By the early 1940s, the SVM was of negligible importance, and a new and different organization of unrelated origin founded in 1936, the Student Foreign Missions Fellowship (SFMF), was coming into its own to fill the gap.

The reasons for the decline of the SVM are not easily bottled into the last paragraph of a short epilogue to a small book, and no such attempt will be made. In an important way, however, the Movement which declined during the 1920s was fundamentally different from the triumphant uprising of the 1880s and 1890s. The first chairman to succeed Mott explained the watchword to the 1924 delegates in a way which would have proved completely foreign to the students of the 1890s: "To evangelize means 'to permeate with the Spirit of the Gospel.' Our purpose is to permeate with the spirit of the Gospel not only individuals, but also society and international relationships."[9] But how does one complete *that* in a generation? And how does one *ever* know when he is finished with such a task? The vision of much of the SVM's leadership had, by the 1920s, changed significantly. The well-outlined sense of purpose the watchword had originally served to focus so vividly now was projected as fuzzy and diffuse. A fascinating question is thus posed for the sociologically oriented (a question of more than just theoretical importance to mission-minded students of the present day): Why was the SVM unable to prevent the erosion of that clearly defined goal which was from the very beginning its most important, nay rather its sole and unrivalled, reason for existence? Was the SVM a victim of a tragic and avoidable organizational flaw, such as the stipulation that its executive committee be chosen by other religious organizations; or was the SVM an inevitable casualty of the changing times? We would leave this question to the student of the movement's decline.

notes

Chapter 1

1. *Missionary Review,* Vol. X. May 1887
2. C.P. Shedd, *Two Centuries of Student Christian Movements,* p. 36.

Chapter 2

1. J.R. Mott, in *Missionary Issues of the Twentieth Century,* p. 272.
2. R.P. Wilder, *The Student Volunteer Movement for Foreign Missions,* (hereafter, *SVMFM),* p. 11.
3. J.R. Mott, op. cit., p. 276.
4. A.T. Pierson, in *Student Mission Power: The Report of the First International Convention of the Student Volunteer Movement for Foreign Missions,* p. 81. (Hereafter convention proceedings will be labeled by the date of the convention, in italics).
5. *1891,* p. 79.
6. J.R. Mott, op. cit. p. 275.
7. R.E. Speer, *What Constitutes a Missionary Call,* p. 13.
8. J.R. Mott, *The Evangelization of the World in This Generation,* p. 22.
9. *1894,* p. 109.
10. J.R. Mott, *Missionary Issues of the Twentieth Century,* p. 274.
11. J.R. Mott, op. cit., p. 276.
12. J.R. Mott, op. cit., p. 282.
13. *1891,* p. 33.

14. Volunteer Keith Falconer, quoted with approval by J.R. Mott, in *1894*, p. 79.
15. R.E. Speer, op. cit., p. 21.
16. *1891*, p. 74.
17. J.R. Mott, *The Evangelization of the World in This Generation*, p. 23.
18. J.R. Mott, in *Twenty-Fifth Anniversary of the Student Volunteer Movement*, p. 2.
19. R.E. Speer, op. cit., p. 10.

Chapter 3

1. C.P. Shedd, op. cit., p. 50 (quoted from Woolbridge).
2. cf. Shedd, op. cit., chapters IV and V, for further information on Samuel J. Mills.
3. Shedd, op. cit., pp. 48-61.
4. W.R. Hogg, *Ecumenical Foundations*, p. 13.
5. Shedd, op. cit., p. 63.
6. Shedd, op. cit., p. 127.
7. L.D. Wishard, *The Students' Challenge to the Churches*, p. 13.
8. Shedd, op. cit., p. 58.
9. Shedd, op. cit., p. 100.
10. For further information on Luther Wishard and the IYMCAM, see Shedd, op. cit., chapters VII-IX.
11. Shedd, op. cit., pp. 157-161.
12. R.W. Braisted, *In This Generation*, pp. 14-15.
13. Wilder, *SVMFM*, p. 9.
14. Wilder, op. cit., pp. 7-8.
15. Shedd, op. cit., pp. 229-231.
16. Shedd, op. cit., pp. 232-237.
17. J.R. Mott in *Christian Students and World Problems*, pp. 52-63; quoted in C.P. Shedd, op. cit., p. 291.
18. B.R. Mathews, J.R. *Mott*, p. 34.
19. Shedd, op. cit., pp. 289-294; B.R. Mathews, op. cit.
20. Shedd, op. cit., chapter XV.
21. Shedd, op. cit., p. 257.
22. Mott [1893], quoted in Shedd, op. cit., p. 260.
23. Quoted J.R. Mott in *Twenty-Fifth Anniversary of the SVM*, p. 11.
24. J.R. Mott, in op. cit., p. 13.
25. Wilder, *SVMFM*, p. 16.
26. Mott, *Addresses and Papers*, v. 1, p. 5.
27. Mott, in *Twenty-Fifth Anniversary of the SVM*, p. 12.
28. Mott, in op. cit., p. 15.

29. Braisted, op. cit., p. 32.
30. Wilder, op. cit., p. 18.
31. Braisted, op. cit., loc. cit.
32. Braisted, op. cit., p. 33.
33. Wilder, op. cit., p. 18.
34. Wilder, op. cit., p. 19.
35. Braisted, op. cit., p. 35.
36. cf. Mott, *Addresses and Papers*, v. 1, p. 7.
37. Mott, op. cit., loc. cit.
38. Mott., op. cit., pp. 2-12.
39. Wilder, in *1891*, p. 164.
40. Mott, op. cit., p. 8.
41. R.D. Winter, private interview.
42. Wilder, op. cit., p. 39.

Chapter 4

1. J.R. Mott [1894], *Addresses and Papers*, v. 1, p. 308.
2. Mott, *Five Decades and a Forward View*, p. 26.
3. Mott, *Addresses and Papers*, v. 1, p. 301.
4. Mott, *The Evangelization of the World in This Generation*, p. 190.
5. *1891*, p. 86.
6. Ibid., p. 173.
7. Ibid.
8. Mott, in *Twenty-Fifth Anniversary of the SVM*, p. 63.
9. For information on the volunteer bands, cf. R.E. Speer, in *1891*, pp. 39-42.
10. cf. J.R. Mott, *Addresses and Papers*, v. 1, pp. 8-10.
11. Ibid., p. 27.
12. Ibid., pp. 176-177.
13. R.D. Winter, *Protestant Mission Societies: The American Experience* (Pasadena, William Carey Library, 1979) pp. 140-141.
14. Statistics in this paragraph taken from *1891*, p. 78.
15. *1906*, p. 43.
16. Mott, *Addresses and Papers*, v. 1, pp. 173-199.
17. *1898*, p. 274.
18. *1898*, p. 201.
19. *1894*, p. 24.
20. Mott, *Five Decades and a Forward View*, p. 23.
21. Mott, *The Evangelization of the World in This Generation*, p. 134.
22. Quoted in Mott, op. cit., p. 134.
23. Mott, *Twenty-Fifth Anniversary of the SVM*, p. 51; *Evangelization of the World in This Generation*, p. 135.

24. *1894*, p. 106.
25. Quoted in Mott, p. 103.
26. R.P. Wilder, *The Great Commission*, p. 84.
27. Op. Cit., p. 84.
28. *1891*, p. 174.
29. *1891*, p. 79, p. 75.
30. *1894*, p. 115.
31. Mott, *Evangelization of the World in This Generation*, chapters IV, V.
32. Speer, in *1891*, p. 77.
33. Mott, *Addresses and Papers*, v. 1, p. 19.
34. Speer, *1891*, p. 77.
35. Mott, *Addresses and Papers*, v. 1, p. 257.
36. Ibid., p. 18.
37. Mott, *Twenty-Fifth Anniversary of the SVM*, p. 266.
38. G. Warneck, *Outline of a History of Protestant Missions*, (New York: Fleming Revell, 1901), p. 102.
39. Mott, *Addresses and Papers*, v. 1, p. 305.
40. Op. cit., pp. 317-323.
41. Op. cit., p. 194.
42. *1924*, p. 64.
43. Mott, *Five Decades and a Forward View*, p. 27; cf. Wilder, quoted in *Missionary Review*, Vol. XIII, Sept. 1892.
44. *1891*, p. 161.
45. Wilder, *SVMFM*, pp. 7-12.
46. *1894*, p. 34.
47. Mott, *Addresses and Papers*, v. 1, p. 12.
48. George Sherwood Eddy, *Eighty Adventurous Years*, (New York: Harper & Brothers, 1955), p. 82.
49. *1891*, p. 47.
50. W.R. Moody, *D.L. Moody*, p. 380.
51. G. Warneck, op. cit., loc. cit.
52. *1894*, p. 68.
53. *1891*, p. 44.
54. Wilder, *SVMFM*, p. 40.

Chapter 5

1. Wilder, *SVMFM*, p. 10.
2. Braisted, op. cit., p. 11.
3. Wilder, *SVMFM*, p. 8.
4. Mott, *Addresses and Papers*, v. 1, p. 358.
5. Nettie Dunn Clark, quoted in Wilder, *SVMFM*, p. 46.

Chapter 6

1. Mott [1920], *Addresses and Papers*, v. 1, p. 176.
2. Ibid.
3. W.R. Hogg, op. cit., p. 35.
4. Mott, *Five Decades and a Forward View*, chapter 11.
5. K.S. Latourette, *History of the Expansion of Christianity*, v. 4, p. 98.
6. Wheeler, *Man Sent From God*, p. 52.
7. *Missionary Herald*, vol. LXXXVII, (April, 1891), p. 138.
8. *Missionary Herald*, vol. CXXXII, (Feb, 1936), p. 87.
9. J.C. Robbins, in *1924*, pp. 84-85.

Bibliography

Material on the Student Volunteer Movement is remarkably difficult to come by, and many of the original sources listed below are likely to be unavailable in the libraries of even the largest universities and seminaries. The one notable exception to this rule is the proceedings of the 1891 Convention, which have recently been republished by the William Carey Library under the name *Student Mission Power*. This is a selective bibliography; I have only listed the materials which contain the most information on the SVM, or those on which I have drawn heavily.

Original Sources

Anonymous, *Report of the First International Convention of the Student Volunteer Movement for Foreign Missions, 1891.* (Republished: South Pasadena, CA, Wm. Carey Library, 1979)

_____, Reports of the Second through the Twelfth Conventions of the Student Volunteer Movement for Foreign Missions. (1894, 1898, 1902, 1906, 1910, 1914, 1920, 1924, 1928, 1932, 1936; 1894 Proceedings pub. by T.O. Metcalf and Co., Boston; others pub. by SVM Press, New York).

_____, *The Missionary Uprising Among the Students* (New York, SVM Press, n.d.)

_____, *Missionary Issues of the Twentieth Century.* (Nashville, Press of the Publishing House M.E. Church, South, 1901).

_____, *The Twenty-Fifth Anniversary of the Student Volunteer Movement,* (New York, SVM Press, 1911).

Mott, John R., *Addresses and Papers of J.R. Mott,* v. 1, *The Student Volunteer Movement for Foreign Missions.* (New York, Association Press, 1946).

_____, *Five Decades and a Forward View,* (New York, Harper and Brothers, 1939).

_____, *The Evangelization of the World in This Generation,* (New York, SVM Press, 1900).

Speer, Robert E., *What Constitutes a Missionary Call.* (pamphlet published many times by the SVM; first published in 1901).

Wilder, Robert P., *The Great Commission,* (London, Oliphants, 1936).

_____, *The Student Volunteer Movement: Its Origin and Early History,* (New York, SVM Press, 1935).

Wishard, Luther D., *A New Programme of Missions,* (New York, Fleming H. Revell, 1895).

_____, *The Students' Challenge to the Churches,* (New York, Fleming H. Revell, 1895).

For further information on the SVM, see also the *Missionary Review of the World* and the *Missionary Herald* for the dates in question.

Pertinent Biographies

Braisted, Ruth Wilder, *In This Generation: The Story of Robert P. Wilder,* (New York, Friendship Press, 1941).

Mathews, Basil J., *John R. Mott, World Citizen.* (New York, Harper and Brothers).

Moody, W.R., *D.L. Moody,* (New York, MacMillan Company, 1930).

Pierson, D.L., *Arthur T. Pierson* (New York, Fleming Revell, 1912).

Wheeler, W. Reginald, *A Man Sent From God, a Biography of Robert E. Speer,* (Westwood, N.J., Fleming H. Revell, 1956).

Secondary Sources on SVM and Related Movements

Hogg, William Richey, *Ecumenical Foundations,* (New York, Harper and Brothers, 1932).

Hopkins, C. Howard, *History of the YMCA in North America,* (New York, Association Press, 1951).

Howard, David M., *Student Power in World Evangelism,* (Downers Grove, Illinois, Inter Varsity Press, 1971).

Orr, J. Edwin, *Campus Aflame,* (Glendale, CA, Gospel Light Publications, 1971).

Rouse, Ruth, *The World's Student Christian Federation: A History of the First Thirty Years,* (London, S.C.M. Press Ltd., 1948).

Shedd, Clarence P., *Two Centuries of Student Christian Movements, Their Origin and Intercollegiate Life* (New York, Association Press, 1934).

Tatlow, Tissington, *The Story of the Student Christian Movement of Great Britain and Ireland* (London, S.C.M. Press, 1933).

About the Author

Timothy C. Wallstrom, A.B., M.S., is a graduate of Stanford University, where he received degrees in both history and physics. Born in Iran, the son of Presbyterian medical missionaries, Mr. Wallstrom spent the first semester of the '79-'80 academic year at the United States Center for World Mission, where he researched and wrote *The Creation of a Student Movement to Evangelize the World.* He is presently at Princeton University studying for a doctorate in physics.